JAN. 2014.

THE

ONLY

WAY

IS

MOTORHOMING

BY JRA VAN DUELLERE

FOR MY DARLING

"Not all those who wander are lost"　-JRR Tolkien

"A ship in a harbour is safe, but that is not what ships are built for"　-John A. Shedd

"The world is a book, and those who do not travel read only a page"　-Saint Augustine

"Don't tell me how educated you are, tell me how much you travelled"　-Mohammed

"I have found out that there aint no surer way to find out whether you like people or hate them, than to travel with them"　-Mark Twain

"For my part, I travel not to go anywhere, but to go. I travel for travel's sake. The great affair is to move."　-Robert Louis Stephenson

"A man of ordinary talent will always be ordinary, whether he travels or not; but a man of superior talent (which I cannot deny myself to be without being impious) will go to pieces if he remains forever in the same place...."　-Wolfgang Amadeus Mozart

"Man cannot discover new oceans unless he has the courage to lose sight of the shore."　-Andre Gide

"Man is an artefact designed for space travel. He is not designed to remain in his present biologic state any more than a tadpole is designed to remain a tadpole." -William S. Burroughs

"Of all possible subjects, travel is the most difficult for an artist, as it is the easiest for a journalist." -W.H. Auden

"It always rains on tents. Rainstorms will travel thousands of miles, against prevailing winds for the opportunity to rain on a tent." -Dave Barry

"Come on John lad, we'll walk on the sunny side of the street" -Richard Harvey

"I hitched a ride with my soul by the side of the road, just as the sky turned black" -N. Gallagher

"And then one day you'll walk right out of this life, and you'll wonder why you didn't try" -P. Weller

"My way or the highway" -D. Fisher

Contents

Foreword

FOREWORD

The places and people you are about to read about are entirely real, although in some cases the names have been changed to protect the innocent and or guilty.

All of the things we did were set up purely for our own entertainment and nothing has been embellished or enhanced.

I truly believe that the only way is motorhoming. One day I think everyone will realise this………….. but for the sake of peace and quiet, I hope not for some time yet.

Chapter 1

SLEDGING

Thursday 17th December 2009

There were only two days to go before our Christmas break began. On Wednesday, I had been looking forward to the prospect of going to the new forest with my darling in our motorhome. Then the phone rang, and my heart sank as I was asked to return to a previous job. There wasn't really two day's work for me to do at Overton, but I had little chance of getting everything done in one day. The company I worked for just needed the job done, and were happy to give me two days wages to make sure the surplus delivery didn't get rendered useless by exposure to the elements over the holiday period.

In keeping with building site etiquette across the country a radio was blaring loudly for communal use, keeping me abreast of an ever worsening weather forecast. I feared that our motorhome may become stuck at the top of the hill we had perched it upon, and would have left immediately were it not for the cost this would incur on the only firm to have given me any work since the recession started. Instead I resolved to work faster for the rest of the day, in the hope I might be able to sail off down to Blissford straight after finishing.

My efforts were in vain, however, and when time came to lock up the site I had to go, leaving a couple of hours work for Friday morning. As I made the short journey home on my trusty scooter snowflakes had already begun to fall, and I wondered whether I would make it back the next day or not. Fortunately the scooter has always performed well in the snow as long as I go slow, and with only a short distance to travel I usually make it to work when most others fail.

After a comfortingly hot shower, I sat down in my armchair with the cup of tea my dearest always has ready for me. It soon became clear we had both heard the same weather forecast as we reaffirmed one another's fears with regards to getting off the hill. All I could do was apologise for having brought us here, as for the sake of two days wages we had both been frustrated at the thought of coming back. The irony in that I may not be able to get there in the morning anyway and would have to leave the job unfinished was palpable. As always the darling displayed a totally calm understanding of my predicament, although how long this understanding would last while stuck in a van on the top of a hill in a snowstorm I was not eager to discover.

The next morning did reveal that there had been a light snowfall during the night, meaning I had to exert caution on the scooter. Tracks in the snow showed that the road had already been used by at least a few vehicles, and as the sun was already making a brave attempt at shining I tried to replace my feeling of impending doom with the more optimistic thought of going to Blissford. If I could manage to get everything done before we had any more snow I knew we would be ok. With more incentive than usual it was easy to work quickly, and having made an early start I was almost finished by 9.30.

The sun had long since gone back to bed when the god of snow entered the conspiracy against us. I had about forty plasterboards still to get undercover when the largest snowflakes I have ever seen began to drift down out of the sky, slowly at first but as the wind picked up they began to swirl round in the air and come heavier. Every time I came back out of the building to get another board there was a scattering of snow on the top one, which had only been uncovered for a matter of seconds. With time being of the essence I had taken the scooter right into the heart of the building site, and with no tools or packed lunch to carry I just jumped right on and set off home as soon as the last board was inside.

On my way up our hill I could see that, in spite of my best efforts, we had been thwarted by the weather, there being no sensible way we could risk driving the van down such an incline. As I reached the top the back wheel of the scooter lurched from side to side as it lost traction on the steep gradient, meaning I had to get off and push the last twenty yards at a snail's pace in constant fear of a vehicle coming round the blind corner at the top.

During the summer we had often been lucky enough to be allowed to camp on the farmers own garden, as opposed to in the field with all the other campers. This was because we came and went quite regularly and would often lose our pitch to a newcomer, so Annie had very kindly said it would be ok. Indeed it was much more than ok from our perspective, providing us with a view across Amos's thirty foot fish pond stocked with koi carp. It all looked quite surreal under a blanketing of snow, the normal farmyard junk being hidden from view as I approached. As I reached the van I noticed vapours rising from the vent on the side, indicating not only that the darling had sympathy for me returning home half frozen, but that she had also given up all hope of going to Blissford.

Undaunted by such a travesty of fate, we settled down to the beginning of our Christmas break and had a couple of glasses of wine that afternoon. Whether by intuition or simply just a female love of shopping the darling had insisted we got to the supermarket in Newbury on Wednesday night as we drove over from Binstead, meaning the cupboards of the van were full to bursting point and we had no immediate need to go anywhere. Knowing how comfortable we can be in the van, we saw it as no big problem to have to sit and wait a couple of days for the roads to become safe again. I could not help but think though, that if I had gotten away from work thirty minutes sooner we would have been safely down the hill where the roads weren't too bad.

Relentlessly the snow continued. The next morning's news informed us that seventy drivers had become trapped and had to spend the night in their cars near Basingstoke, a distance of about ten miles from where we were. I went outside for a smoke after breakfast and could see well over a foot of snow on the van roof, showing at least that the van was well insulated and we were not losing any of our precious heat, and I immediately felt sympathy for anyone who had spent the night in such a manner with nothing but the protection afforded by an ordinary vehicle.

We had managed to keep our spirits up at first, thinking that in a few days the horrible stuff would have melted and the van would be free to take us wherever we wanted to go once again. The following Monday was the twenty first of December, and far from relenting the snow had continued to return in sporadic bursts. No sooner did we see a brief thaw than a fresh snowstorm would arrive that night, engulfing the whole of the hill in a fresh white fluffy blanket of snow. The trouble was that we had started to run low on all the perishable items I would usually pick up in the shop on my way home from work, such as bread and milk and of course tobacco.

Amos and Annie had been very sympathetic to our plight, saying that if there was anything we needed we had only to ask, but Christmas being what it is I needed some alcohol and dear old Annie and Amos didn't drink. At the end of the farmyard lane I prepared to set off down the hill on the scooter when at the last moment I saw a car on its side by the road. Clearly the owner had managed to get out and was hoping to return to the car when the snow had gone, there being no possible way that it could be moved as things were.

I left the bike idling and walked to the top of the hill. As I tentatively edged round the blind corner I immediately realised that unless I was prepared to walk across the fields in a couple of feet of snow, then I faced a Christmas without wine, cigars or chocolate and any of the other small luxuries which make that time of year what it is. I turned the bike around and headed back to the van, more cautiously now having seen a crumpled car in the dyke. I told the darling what I had seen and that I had decided to walk across the fields to Kingsclere. We both knew the pathways quite well by now, and I would at least be safe from traffic.

After a round trip of about five miles I returned home with a rucksack full of everything we had been able to think of, from mince pies and television guide's to leek's and wines. I had found the last quarter of the journey extremely difficult, having to climb a very steep incline in deep snow, with the knowledge that veering off the path to either side could result in a twisted ankle. Not wanting to think about it too much I had pushed onwards, eventually reaching home about two hours after I had set out. With the heating on in the van we have a ready supply of hot water, so as soon as I was through the door I got my wet clothes off and had a shower. From the comfort of my armchair it almost felt as if I hadn't been anywhere.

Aside from us there had been two other couples on the camp site in the run up to Christmas, both of them in caravans. They had both left to go and stop in a nearby hotel from what I could gather. One of them had been quick to sing the virtues of all things caravanning while telling me he used to have a motorhome but got rid of it, a common enough story that I have heard from many caravanners. The other guy had told me one day that he could deal with having no water coming into the van, referring to the fact that his water supply was frozen, but when he found himself unable to pour anything down the sink because the plugholes were frozen he'd had enough. Thankfully we faced no such problems and, in spite of the fact it sat covered in over a foot of snow, the van was more than equal to the task.

The outdoor tap from which we got our water had long since frozen solid, meaning that I had to lift a manhole cover and use a standpipe, as Amos's son Joe must have done each morning for the livestock. A couple of days before Christmas things became too cold even for the standpipe, no doubt creating all sorts of problems for the farm. Annie very kindly allowed me to fill some large bottles in her kitchen, and although I had to make numerous journeys I managed to fill the tank. As I filled the last bottles Annie then took kindness to a new level, handing me a basket and proceeding to fill it with food. The television was on in the corner but was going unnoticed by Amos, who sat in front of it warming his feet at the fire. Wearing the same happy expression I never saw him without he simply said, "loike mince pies?" to which I could only nod before he continued, "Box o mince pies o'er there".

Obviously Amos and Annie had spent many years at the farm and seen their share of harsh winters, leaving them oblivious to the sense of isolation that had descended upon me and my dearest. Fortunately we had at least chosen the right place to get stuck I thought, as I watched the basket filling with duck eggs and goose eggs along with various items from the freezer. In the course of conversation I learnt that until very recently Amos had been responsible for keeping the hill free of snow, but the council now refused to pay him to do so, probably in the hope he would do it anyway. As I was about to leave he went on to say that if I ran short of gas there was a bottle in the yard I could use, and in this he answered my prayers for I had noticed that our supply had indeed begun to run low. Our heating is very efficient and we use only a little gas, but we had not accounted for the possibility of being stranded for so long.

With our fresh supplies we enjoyed a happy Christmas, safe in the knowledge that we had enough gas and that I could get more food from Annie if need be. The couple of day's work I had returned here for had cost us dearly. We had at first told ourselves it would only be a couple of days and we would be able to get down from the hill, and now over a week later we were still there. This did not in the least resemble what we had planned for our Christmas break. Although I knew from the news that the whole of the country had seen snow, to this day I remain firmly of the opinion that had we been able to leave a few hours earlier we would have been ok. If we had got stuck in the New Forest we would at least have had a pub and a shop on site.

The last few months at work had been strenuous to say the very least, the thought of taking the forest walks we had so much enjoyed the previous Christmas being the only thing at times that had kept us going. Feeling that we had to try and salvage something from the holiday period, we walked out to the top of the hill the next morning to see if it was possible to get down. It was now Boxing Day and with more snow forecast it felt like a case of now or never. At least someone had managed to remove the car from the dyke, implying that a reasonably large vehicle had made the journey safely at least once. Edging round the blind corner we could see that the tarmac of the road had begun to peek through what remained of the snow. A slight dip in the road prevented us from seeing all the way down, but it had obviously been used by at least a few vehicles.

We both wanted to go somewhere different for the last week of our break. We had found our surroundings to be a beautiful place during the summer but, possibly because we were quite high up, the snow would not budge from the fields rendering a walk impossible. We looked down the hill and then looked at one another, at which point I made myself as positive and encouraging as I possibly could. It must have took us ten minutes to walk back to the van and a further five minutes while we got ready to move, with me fastening my scooter to the back of the van.

But for one stubborn patch of snow beneath the overhanging trees, we made our way out of the farm quite easily. Annie and Amos knew that we might leave at any moment, and we had already said our farewells knowing that I would be back in a week. At the edge of the lane my darling drew the van to a halt while we sat a moment and contemplated what we were about to do. My biggest fear was not being able to stop at the bottom, where the road came to a tee junction enabling us to go left to Overton or right to Kingsclere. I knew from experience on my way to and from work that drivers would pass there at about fifty miles an hour, with no chance of seeing what came down the hill until it poked its front bumper into view from behind the large hedges at either side.

I could see that the darling was having second thoughts as I was myself. We knew that we had to do it though, the only alternative now being to reverse back down the tight lane into the farm as it would be impossible to turn around even without the snow. The van would screech with the pain of the overhanging branches when we travelled forwards, there was no way we would try it in reverse. Looking at each other we both wondered what we were doing. I unfastened my seat belt, fully expecting to have to get out and watch from behind as we reversed along the lane, when a look of steely resolve mixed with resignation came across my darlings face. She muttered an expletive and the van lurched forwards.

Before we had even rounded the blind corner I could tell that we were moving faster than the darling would have been happy with. I felt a moment of anxiety as I realised I had not refastened my seat belt then forgot about it altogether as the back end of the van started moving to one side. We were now in the unprecedented position of travelling sideways down the hill, a view of the dyke which should have been to our left hand side now rushing past the windscreen. I knew that, because of the gradient of the hill, we could easily end up with the van on its side in the dyke, and so wasted no time at all in jumping from my armchair and running to the back of the van.

With the brakes on we had managed to slow down but could not stop. The darling did not want me to get out -and said so- but I quickly explained that I would have to get out at the bottom, in order to try and stop the traffic on the other road which cut across us. I suggested opening her window so I could hear her shouting at me, then bailed out of the back door and into the relative safety of the snow and ice.

My feet slipped in all directions beneath me, but with difficulty I managed to remain upright. With the van still sliding slowly down the hill at a peculiar angle, I braced my feet in the gutter which was to our right as we looked down the hill. I tried to push the back end of the van round, wanting the rear wheels to follow the same path as the front ones, but the weight of the van just pushed me further in to the dyke. I began to panic, not only because we were facing the prospect of the van being stuck in the dyke until god knows when, but more importantly my darling was still inside. I replanted my feet in the gutter hoping for more grip, and decided to push right at the back of the van where the added leverage may help my cause.

Banishing my fears of being crushed by a capsized motorhome, I pushed with all the strength I could muster, and at last the van began to realign its self. There had been a distinct lack of commands issued from the window of the van, which was now picking up speed again in an attempt to remain straight. More sliding than running I tried to keep up, and quickly realised what the darling was doing. The small dip in the road which prevented us from seeing the bottom of the hill was now in front of us, and if we didn't hit it with enough speed we might not get up the other side and so be stuck in a blind dip on what had become almost a ski slope. Breathlessly trying to catch up, I could see the front wheels of the van spinning on the compacted snow as the darling tried to make it to the summit.

By the time I caught up the van was sat at the top of the next hill, looking down toward the tee junction about a quarter of a mile away. I asked if the darling was ok, receiving a cold stare that conveyed just how incredulous a question she thought that had really been. I seem to remember offering to take over behind the wheel but this is vehemently disputed, forever afterwards the occasion being referred to as and I quote, "that time you pushed me off a cliff in a three and a half tonne sledge".

I tried to make sure that the van at least stayed straight, but was aware that I had to be the first to reach the bottom or she would just plough into the traffic coming from either side. About two hundred yards from the junction the van began to snake from side to side again, and I felt a sickening feeling rising from my stomach. With luck the darling managed to bring her under control, using the gutter to our left as a brake she ground to a halt, giving me a chance to get ahead and do my traffic warden impression.

Just as we had started to get the situation under control it became a bit more complicated. Staying in the gutter in the vague hope I might be able to remain on my feet, I thought all I had to do was stop the traffic and we would manage the last two hundred yards easily. With complete dismay I heard a voice behind me, telling me I could not stop where I was and would have to keep going. Wondering who could be so short of intelligence that they were unable to see we had no intention of stopping there, but were merely trying to get down cautiously, I turned around.

The car looked as expensive as the accent had sounded, and with regards to intelligence my finger had been right on the button. For some unknown reason, probably obscure even to himself, this person had seen fit to get out of his car and walk ten yards down the hill toward me. As I looked at him I could see that his car behind him had started to slide sideways down the hill, regardless of the handbrake being on. With his wife and kids screaming at him he made a desperate attempt to get back in, displaying all the co-ordination of a newly born calf on an ice rink.

I knew that my darling could see how desperate the state of affairs had just become and that we had no time to waste. I fell over a couple of times myself, and for a moment I contemplated sliding down the hill on my back in an attempt to get to the junction first, but would need to get in front of the van before it was worth trying. In my desperation to overtake I got into the gutter again. My ankle twisted on something uneven, probably frozen mud refusing to accommodate my footing, but my adrenaline refused to let me feel the pain. With only seconds to spare I managed to reach the junction and stop the traffic, averting a sure collision.

As my darling turned the van towards Kingsclere I opened the door and jumped back inside, and have never been so relieved to get back in my armchair.

Chapter 2

THE HILTON, MALTA.

Shortly before Christmas, 2001.

A black SUV had dispatched us and our luggage at the grandiose steps of the Hilton, within an hour or so of arriving at Malta airport. The attack on the world trade centre had happened some eight weeks previously, and as this had been my first time on an aeroplane I wanted to put the experience behind me. My darling's heels clicked on the marble floor of the foyer, keeping me awake as we made the seemingly endless journey to the desk at the far side. It was well after midnight by the time we made it to our room. In the process of exploring our new living quarters and patio we made a bit too much noise, drawing vocal protests from above.

Needless to say, this being a brand new five star Hilton, everything was more than perfect. Even the slightly suggestive glance of the waitress as she led us to our breakfast table the next morning, calling me Mr Smith when I suspect she knew this not to be the case, was not in the least abrasive but more like a welcome break from the formality that comes with a five star hotel.

Further exploration revealed there to be an outdoor hot tub only yards from our patio door, ours being a ground floor room. It was partially concealed by some very neat and tidy bushes which somehow managed not to get any of their dead leaves into the water, or else someone meticulously cleaned them out on a regular basis. After a rigorous workout in the hotel gym we spent a couple of hours ensconced in the hot bubbling water, just our heads poking above the surface as we looked out on a sunny but breezy day.

I almost killed our conversation stone dead, when I remarked that I didn't care if it rained because I was so warm in the water, and received at once a very darting look that said my darling was now resigning herself to the heavens opening. Surrounded by such luxury it rarely takes long for a reconciliation, and within moments I was seemingly forgiven as her attention refocused itself on the more pressing matter of keeping her hair out of the water.

Lying back in the water and watching the palm trees swaying in a breeze which was growing in strength, a feeling of serenity descended on me. I'm a glass half full type of person, as opposed to a glass half empty, but nevertheless, whenever on holiday I cannot refrain from counting the amount of days we have left before returning to normal life. Being that this was our first day, this was a safe subject of conversation. One thing leads to another and soon we were discussing the possibility of taking a somewhat lengthier vacation.

Various acquaintances over the years have told me of their foreign holidays, and never having been abroad I had been keen to see what all the fuss was about. I always find myself disheartened though, when I think of working all year just to afford two weeks in the sun, like my whole existence would be for my employers benefit. When I put this to my other half the dear girl surprised me, saying that she would like to live in a motorhome and go travelling. Prior to having met her I had scarcely left my hometown, so I was apprehensive of the idea if I'm honest, but nevertheless a seed had been planted without my even realising it.

We both lay back in the water looking up at what had become quite a grey sky, the palm trees blowing around crazily on the edge of my vision like something from Hawaii five o. When the rain that I had inadvertently wished upon us did arrive, we lay there a few minutes longer, enjoying the sharp contrast of the water falling on our faces with the warmth of the spa. Ten paces and a quick jump over a small balcony later, we were back in our room getting ready to go out for our evening meal.

Forever afterwards I am reminded of this holiday by the smell of Joop, an aftershave I had purchased in duty free on the way out, and on this particular evening I had applied it quite liberally. In contrast to the previous evening the hotel was now quite busy as we made our way into one of the bars, an array of astrological symbols decorating the walls and ceiling in a more tasteful manner than any description could do justice. I was so taken with the place that I insisted we returned there after our meal. Our conversation soon returned to my darling's declaration that she would consider living full time in a motorhome, on the condition, of course, that we had regular holidays in the sun.

I soon began to realise the conviction of her statement, which came as something of a shock for I had considered her far too reluctant to give up all the usual feminine comforts such as hair straighteners and hour long soaks in the bath every night. Leaving me somewhat lost for words she soon decided to head back to our room, claiming exhaustion from the previous days travelling. While I pondered the suggestion she had put to me I had a couple more pints of Black Velvet from the bar, genuine Black velvet that is made with Guinness and Champagne as opposed to the Cider which I would have made do with at home. Only when we came to check out at the end of the holiday did I discover that each pint had cost in excess of fifteen pounds.

Returning home at a time when Sarah Beeny was at the pinnacle of her television career and on our screens at least once a week, it seemed like the whole of England was obsessed with owning a postage stamp size piece of the country and fencing it off, an

14

Englishman's home being his castle etc. Consequently it did not take long to come up with a plan. Within a short period of time we had put together a small library of motorhome magazines. Neither of us had ever set foot in a motorhome or for that matter done anything more than looked longingly at one in the street as it passed by. Seeing one parked up was a small luxury as it was almost possible to build up a mental image of what it would be like to be inside. There was always a reluctance though, to get too close, knowing the owner might be nearby or even inside. As there are no dealerships in Cumbria the only logical solution was to go to one of the country's many motorhome shows.

And so it was that some months later we found ourselves in our little Peugeot on the way to York racecourse, venue of the annual motorhome show there. This took us well outside of our jurisdiction, as until that time if we ever ventured out of sleepy Cumbria it was usually by train en route to an airport or such like, although the aforementioned Peugeot was a veteran of many localised Sunday jaunts. After a few pleasant and rather scenic laps of York we managed to find our destination, following the large number of camping vehicles on the road as opposed to my skill as a navigator.

With the car parked in the field adjoining the showground we had to weave our way through a few hundred camper vans just to get to the entrance, as many of the people who visit are doing so over a few days and therefore camp on site. We paid our entrance fee at the gate, receiving a wristband each and a dollop of ink on the back of our hands. I could now look at the vehicles with impunity, free from the feeling that I was staring at someone's home, however temporary. This was my first real look inside a motorhome and I remember the utter despair I felt as I realised upon entering each one that it was completely unsuitable as a full time home, with the obvious exception of a forty foot juggernaut parked near the entrance. Hence we both felt slightly dejected as we returned back to the Peugeot for our packed lunch.

Having eaten we found it more interesting to sit and watch the mass exodus of assorted camping outfits. This being a Sunday and so the last day of the show, all the campers were leaving and a wide and varied range of vehicles filed past us, many of which were self-built conversions. The problem with much of what we had seen was the internal layout. It was not that what we desired did not exist, rather that most examples also incorporated aspects which we found unfavourable. It is not so easy to change the layout of a vehicle as it is to move the sofa around your house until you get it right.

Of course if you have unlimited funds you can buy that juggernaut you will undoubtedly come across as soon as you walk into almost any one of the numerous shows in the camping merchandise calendar. No doubt you can even employ someone to drive it for you before selling it on at a loss when you tire of it. If you follow my advice though, you will refrain from parting with money at a show as you will probably succumb to the spiel of a sales person rather than make the perfect choice.

The truth of the matter is that what you want is most definitely out there, but that you need to think long and hard about what you want as opposed to what you think you want, and also be honest with yourself about what you can do without. Life in a van is minimal in the way that you have no room for clutter. Indeed this is one of the plus points for many people, me included, for it can be quite liberating and cleansing to rid yourself of things you don't really need. Even if you do find your own special Tardis you will not have room for everything you wish to carry. Believe it or not I actually set off carrying my own barbell and weights. I used them a couple of times, once a very memorable occasion on

Weston Supermare beach, then, having carried them around for a few thousand miles, I saw sense and gave them away.

Back home to our luxurious flat in the heart of the Lake District then. Although it was relatively small it still had so much space which we did not use, yet cost us money. Heating was expensive for example, and also council tax and of course management centre fees, the latter being a fund which all residents were required to pay in to yet only a chosen few it seemed ever got the benefit of. Before I sound resentful of the situation I should say that they showed a remarkable amount of good timing in deciding to repaint the exterior of the building just in time for us to sell up and sail into the sunset. This, you see, was how we financed the purchase of our motorhome. It was a huge leap of faith at the time but looking back I have always said that I shudder at the thought of how close we came to backing out and not actually doing it at all.

In the end we left the flat four years to the day after moving in. I have always read great significance into coincidences, to be honest I think it is true to say that no such thing really exists and the term is a name given by us to any similar sequence of events for which we have no better explanation.

Chapter 3

DAY TRIP TO BELGIUM

With funds sitting in the bank from the sale of our flat, we were in truth no closer to knowing exactly what we wanted by way of a van. Thankfully my darling's sister had very kindly allowed us the use of a small cottage she let out as a holiday home, for a nominal fee of course. We gave away the possessions which we could not sell, and a car boot sale had been necessary to get rid of the things we couldn't bear to throw out, yielding a worthwhile return for a mornings work. When we rolled into the small village of Kirkland in our trusty Peugeot, the boot was crammed to capacity with all our worldly goods.

In no time at all we were very comfortable in the quaint little cottage, which although tiny was infinitely bigger than the home we were aspiring towards. The staircase resembled a ladder to which someone had fitted a carpet, and the upstairs floor was probably smaller than many loft conversions. In some ways this added to the comfort, and we began to get a sense of how it would feel to live in such cramped conditions permanently.

Our collection of motorhome magazines strewn around us we continued to pore over the various articles, making a list of dealerships which appeared reputable at the same time. From the beginning I had set my heart on an American RV, thinking the more living space the better, but when we debated the subject I always found myself having to concede the rather obvious point that, the larger the vehicle, the greater the difficulty in driving. My darling pointed out rather blatantly that this would restrict our options with regards to camp site availability, not to mention fuel consumption, and on that note the matter was usually settled.

On the subject of towable caravans, neither of us had ever shown a great deal of enthusiasm. Not that I have anything against them, more that I have never seen one as being a realistic option for a full time home. They involve far too much fuss for someone who wants to move about on a regular basis, as my line of work in construction can often entail. And so the only thing we really knew at the time was that we wanted a small European style motorhome, which was not exactly narrowing the search criteria down by any significant amount.

In the classified adverts at the back of a magazine I stumbled across contact details for a guy who offered to import the vehicle of your choice, for less money than it would cost from a UK dealer. Wondering how he found this possible, I gave him a ring. He offered an explanation by way of saying he had an import license, but after a short telephone conversation I felt no further enlightened. It wasn't really an option anyway, the obvious downside to the arrangement being that I would not be able to check the vehicle out before purchasing it.

I had only entertained the idea to begin with due to a dis-enchantment with UK dealerships. Those we had visited in the preceding months had fallen well short of impressing us. If we had entered a car showroom with so much money to spend we would have been given five star treatment. In contrast, ninety percent of the places we visited just weren't interested in our custom. Or perhaps they didn't believe we had money to spend and thought we were just there for the fun of looking round, being slightly younger than most of their regular clients. As a result we found it difficult to get many of our questions answered.

I threw my magazine to one side and was reaching for another one from the pile stacked in front of us, when my darling drew our conversation back to the phone call I had made a few moments ago. She had in her hand a magazine, opened at the page of a very glossy advert. I had a tendency to skip past the adverts of dealerships, preferring instead to browse through the classifieds of second hand vans in the hope of finding a bargain.

I had to admit that she had a valid point. Since I had hung the phone up it had been niggling at me as well. There was no reason why we could not do exactly what the guy had offered to do for us, albeit at a cost, and my dearest had obviously been thinking along the same lines. The glossy advert she brandished toward me was for a dealership in Belgium. We intended to spend at least a few months of the year outside of the UK anyway, and so in some ways a left hand drive vehicle could have as many benefits as drawbacks.

In large letters across the aforementioned glossy advert, there was emblazoned a claim to have over a hundred second hand vans along with a wide range of new vehicles. I rang the number at the bottom of the page and was relieved to hear that the guy spoke good English. After a couple more phone calls to ascertain train and ferry times, we realised we could set off the next morning.

Shameful now to admit but we never did the place justice really. Belgium I mean not the dealership. The dealership was a complete waste of time. Of course they had the usual top of the range brand new vehicles on show, along with a forecourt full of second hand models, most of which had seen better days. Also, however, there was a small section of the compound out back which was fenced off. It contained about thirty or so two year old vans, some of which caught our eye immediately.

On approaching them we were quickly accosted by a member of staff, telling us in no uncertain terms that those vans were not for sale. Assuming that he meant they had been sold I was a little puzzled, as a moment ago he had spoken reasonably good English. Feeling slightly frustrated that we had come all the way to a foreign country I asked if he meant they were sold, at which point he re-iterated that we were not allowed to look. Instantly I thought of the bloke whose advert had offered to import a vehicle for us. Obviously when money is changing hands some slightly less than legitimate practises will often occur.

Upon leaving the store we got a taxi straight back to the ferry port and re boarded probably the very same ferry we had just alighted from about four hours or so previously. I honestly can't even say with any degree of certainty which part of Belgium this was, such is the haste with which we were both keen to put the episode behind us. To this day I have never been so happy to return to the green and pleasant land as I was that rather dull and grey morning on which we found ourselves in hull.

The food provided on-board had left a great deal to be desired and my darling had decided not to touch it. Indeed I myself hadn't bothered with the breakfast, so we made locating a decent café our primary objective. With our stomachs by now beginning to rumble we were in no mood to be fussy. A full English breakfast was what our hearts desired and we found this in one of the numerous greasy spoons dotted along the high street.

At risk of sounding like someone who just likes reading magazines, the next step was to buy more magazines. Really we just purchased the new monthly editions of our usual choice and went to a more comfortable looking café we had seen on the way to the newsagent. Sitting there drinking coffee while we made a list of the nearest dealerships, I could see the girl behind the counter paying us no attention whatsoever. Very politely I asked if there was a copy of the yellow pages I could borrow, and having little else to do as the café was very quiet she produced one a few moments later. My darling prides herself on an ability to exploit offers, and after a few phone calls had arranged to hire a car for the next few days at a very reasonable price.

First we went to a small dealership in a place called Deepcar on the outskirts of Sheffield, rather imaginatively called Deepcar Motorhomes International. It sounds much grander than it is or rather was, the recession having laid it to rest very recently. By now our mental image of what we wanted was getting stronger, although I think it's true that you don't really know until you see it. And see it we certainly did. A Hymer B584, referred to in magazines as "the much sought after bar version". Four years old at the time and in the prime of her life.

Perfect in just about every way in fact. So much so that my darling just sat there on the sofa while I inspected an identical model parked alongside that was ten years older, simply because I didn't want to part with such a large amount of cash. Eventually it dawned on me that my dearest had done nothing since we arrived but sit on the sofa inside this van, and we had been there now for at least ten minutes.

However, we did not buy that day. Instead we got back in the car and visited all the local dealers, there being quite a few decent small dealerships in the area at the time. We saw nothing else really of note though, certainly nothing which could compare to the Hymer we had just seen. Parked up next to a golf course in Huddersfield, we ate some chips from the local chippy, and decided that since we had the hire car we might as well head further south.

It had been a very long day though, and so first we went to a holiday inn about halfway down for an overnight stop. The next morning we were up and about early, and soon we were once again wandering round the forecourt of what turned out to be a rather large dealer with some very good vans in stock. Needless to say though, we saw nothing quite as good as what we had just driven away from.

Chapter 4

THE MUCH SOUGHT AFTER BAR VERSION

From a position of uncertainty I had now graduated to knowing exactly what we wanted. My darling insisted, however, on what she termed a cooling off period. So after a week of deliberation during which we both moved in with my mother (where we were waited on hand and foot to the point of being spoilt), we at last made up our minds for certain and set off back down to Deepcar. Knowing we would not be able to take the van that day we set off in the trusty Peugeot.

One thousand pounds deposit was enough to secure the purchase of the van of our dreams and also to ask for a couple of small modifications, namely a cycle carrier on the back for two mountain bikes and a power converter which enables us to get 240 volts from two 12 volt leisure batteries. We also had to have an immobiliser and a category one alarm fitted for insurance purposes, all of which Deepcar Motorhomes International were more than happy to undertake for us.

As good as my mother's hospitality can be it was still difficult to wait the week which Deepcar said they required for our modifications. After what seemed like an eternity we were on our way back down to Sheffield, this time in another hire car as we knew we were collecting the van. We arrived there about midday, and after a substantial credit transaction we were given a brief guided tour before our tour guide stopped the traffic for us and sent us on our way.

I remember thinking at the time that we didn't seem to be adequately informed on many of the vans features, especially since it did not come with an instruction manual but rather a huge tome. In the fullness of time though, I have realised that it simply could not have been any other way, there was just too much to learn and we would have to do it ourselves by trial and error. After all this is essentially a home on wheels, and for us it combined the two biggest items most people will buy in their life in one fell swoop.

Having a small number of points on my driving license it had turned out to be difficult for me to get insurance. So after years of driving a one litre Peugeot, my darling now had to graduate to a twenty foot long, three and a half tonne rolling house. Within a week she had become so proficient that to this day I have never drove our pride and joy, except for once in a large car park to save her from getting wet in the rain when she had just come out of Asda. I was severely chastised for this and have since left the driving to her good self. To begin with I was slightly jealous to be honest, having quite got my head around the idea of being the captain of my very own ship. I do believe though that I got the best end of the bargain, as I get free rein to enjoy the scenery from the high vantage point that our van offers the occupants of the cab.

At this point I should probably describe our new toy. We were now the proud owners of a Hymer B584 with a drop down bed. For anyone unfamiliar with the term, this is a bed fixed to the roof of the vehicle in the driver's cab, which pulls down from the ceiling to a height much lower than a Luton overcab. It takes literally a second to prepare in the evening, in contrast to some sort of arrangement whereby you have to alter the sofas as you get with many caravans, yet at the same time stores completely out of the way when not in use.

Once upon a time I imagined myself having forty winks in the fixed bed at the back while my darling drove us down the m6, but in reality this would never have been practical. Consequently the two things you can never do at the same time in a motorhome are sleep and drive, so a fixed bed at the back simply uses up far too much valuable living space. I do however sleep in the passenger seat whenever we go further than a few miles, a subject of much consternation on the part of my darling who only ever seems to sound the horn when I have slept too long and assistance is required with regards to navigation.

Our cab seats are made by Isringhausen. We have three, two in the cab and one behind, separated from the driver's seat by a table (which we find more than adequate as a dinner table and also as a bedside table when the bed is down). The layout of our van allows us both to sit in an armchair with our feet on the sofa and the table between us, the rear seat having a drinks cabinet adjacent being the reason for the name of bar version. It is this third chair which makes all the difference, not having to both sit in the cab if we want an armchair as you see some couples doing, as they are far superior to any sort of sofa you will find in a caravan. The main advantage being that you can adjust the height and positioning and also recline them almost to lying back proportions if you so require.

Further towards the back we have a cupboard on which we place the television in the evening and which also serves for storage of our electric oven during transit. The opposing side, behind the third chair, we have a wardrobe and then the wet room. The wet room is so called because as well as having a toilet and a sink, it also has a shower in the far corner of the van. After drawing across the shower screen you are provided with a moderately large shower. Right at the very back of the van is situated the kitchen sink, fridge and food cupboards etc.

All contained in a vehicle twenty feet long which means we have never failed to gain access to any camp site we have visited, many of which have been of the certificated location variety more commonly known as cl's which can have very restricted access due to being farmyards and suchlike. First of all though, we returned yet again to my mother's house where we spent the night parked on the road outside. And this is where the van was to remain for almost a fortnight as we slowly moved all our worldly possessions onboard, at least those which we had decided to keep anyway.

We still had the trusty Peugeot, which we now parked at a busy layby with a sign saying £900 in the window. Within a couple of days the car was sold and we spent the proceeds on a new portable tv for the van and a microwave convection combination oven. Still it was almost a fortnight before we actually left my mam's house, a subject of much amusement to my brother and one or two of his friends.

Although my mother's hospitality remains second to none, looking back now I suppose we just weren't ready to leave and after all we had been through to get to this point I think we were just plucking up courage. This may sound silly as there was absolutely no turning back now anyway, but I must point out that, until that time, whenever we had left Cumbria it had been to also leave the country and England was very much unchartered waters for the both of us. I for one really did not know what to expect.

We had recently joined the Uks two main camping clubs, the caravan club and the caravan and camping club, but in the first couple of years when we were still new to the van we went to great lengths to avoid using either, possibly because they can be so expensive and we had paid so much money for a vehicle which contained everything we needed anyway. When we did manage to break away from my mothers the first camp site we ever visited was a certificated location in Allonby near Maryport, about fifteen miles away from my mother's house.

We had slept in the van every night since purchasing it, but due to my mother's hospitality we had spent very little time inside not actually driving or sleeping. Within no time at all we were very comfortably sat down watching "Desperate Housewives", at the time was only in its early stages (about the second series I think). It turned out to be a rather stormy night. Allonby being right on the coast, we thought at times that we were going to capsize. Although we had paid for two nights, the following night saw us parked up on Whitehaven dockside. Sheltered from the wind by some very high walls, we were just a stone's throw away from where my grandfather and grandmother grew up. Writing this now it seems that we did not really want to leave, but we were soon to embark on a journey which has seen us return only briefly to Cumbria in the last seven years.

Chapter 5

MAIDEN VOYAGE

Speaking as someone who hails from one of the most beautiful parts of England, I think it is true to say that no matter how nice your surroundings are, at some point they become considerably less than exciting when you see them every single day. I have very fond memories of driving round the lakes on Sunday afternoons, sometimes after a Sunday lunch in a good pub but more often than not after a packed lunch eaten in our trusty Peugeot whilst parked in one of the numerous areas of outstanding natural beauty. On the way home we would often stop in Grasmere, where I would treat myself to a packet of Sara Nelson's Grasmere ginger bread (other brands of gingerbread are available), for which there would often be a queue stretching along the pavement and past the churchyard next door.

Having all this on our doorstep, does, I believe, go at least a small way to excusing us for not having ventured out of Cumbria all that often. Indeed, up until getting the van I had only been to Scotland a couple of times in my life even having lived only forty miles from the border for some thirty odd years. Consequently we now made this our next destination. In fact I like to think of it as our maiden voyage, which in tannie it was if you disregard the journey back to Cumbria from Deepcar, and a couple of other short journeys to show off the van to friends and family.

In my opinion Cumbria is, however, vastly overrated. To me it seems almost to have been a small part of Scotland which at some point in time us English have stolen just so that we could have some loch's as well, changing their name to lakes in the process. To say the very least Scotland is at least as beautiful as the Lake District, and there is so much more of it. Ok so some city centres are probably places the average tourist would be best advised to stay away from, but from what I have seen Scotland is like the lakes from top to bottom, with the added bonus of being slightly more motorhome friendly.

Our first night in this foreign land was spent in Castle Douglas, a place we had visited a few times in the past, in a small car park carefully chosen on account of its proximity to the tourist information office. Bearing in mind this was seven years ago, and I cannot with any degree of certainty say that this would still be the case, but upon entering the tourist information office the next morning I was told the car park was free. I also collected an assortment of leaflets concerning local camp sites, one of which being Carlingwark loch which is ran by the local council, where we planned to stay the next night.

And so after a quick walk into town to pick up a few things which we still had not got round to buying, namely a kettle and a lighter for the gas hob, we made our way to the camp site. I was told on arrival that I would be entitled to a discount in the local gym as it was also council owned, and would very much have liked to give this a go. Due to health and safety however, I would still have needed to do an induction course, and as we only intended a short stay in the area I thought it not to be worth the effort and opted instead for a walk round the lake with my darling, this being an area which the health and safety police have thankfully left alone for the moment.

A couple of days later we were off again. One short drive through some rather majestic scenery later, we pulled in to Brighouse bay, the entrance to which is menacingly overlooked by an old R.A.F jet. After a quick workout in the sites own gym, (inclusive with the price of the pitch), we were out walking again. To say that we walked through some woods and down to the water's edge does not quite do the experience justice though, and the area really needs to be seen to be believed.

That evening we were witness to an event which I found strange at the time, but which in later years has come to epitomise caravanning for me. It had been quite a pleasant day, I remember it well as it was my darling's birthday, and we sat out in our deck chairs and enjoyed a few small glasses of wine into the early evening. As can be the case in Scotland however, the weather was by no means tropical.

Although we were quite some way short of a gale there was now something considerably more than a light breeze whipping up so we retreated into the van. It was with great amazement that we then saw one of our neighbours striding out across the open field with a table in his hands. He proceeded to set two places with knives, forks and glasses etc., before being joined by his wife and enjoying his evening meal. Suffice to say though, that I have witnessed this sort of behaviour now on quite a number of occasions, and consider myself immune to the eccentricities of your average caravanner.

A few days later we moved on again, this time heading for Stirling Castle. An important point to make about visiting such attractions with a motorhome, is that it is always best to make a quick telephone call first and check if the car park can accommodate you, as many can have height barriers. Due to their very nature though, castles usually have quite substantial car parks. As a member of the national trust I have been to many such locations with our van and have never really had much difficulty. For me this is a very pleasurable pass time, as I love all the historic houses our country has to offer.

Weather permitting, we usually have a walk round the gardens when we first arrive, then return to the van for lunch, and so escape the extortionate prices these places charge for refreshments in their cafe or restaurant. Then, fully fed and watered, we will proceed to the house or castle for a stroll around the main attractions. Stirling Castle however, leaves much to be desired and at risk of upsetting some of our patriotic friends from across the border I can only say that if there is anything there worth seeing, I must have missed that part.

A much more worthy destination is the nearby Wallace monument, which is where we went to next. The car park was less spacious but my darling still managed to get us parked up even though there were quite a few people already there when we arrived. A bus is available to help those with less energy make their way to the top of the hill where the monument stands proudly looking out across the valley below, personally I prefer the climb up the hill to being squashed inside a minibus. At the top we found the views to be quite remarkable to say the least. Also on display is a sword, which, it is claimed, belonged to William Wallace, the great Scottish warrior made famous by Mel Gibson in Braveheart.

There are many such places to visit in Scotland and I could quite happily have spent the rest of my life driving from one to the next, if funds would allow it. However, this was not the case and our thoughts were now turning to our finances and getting back to work. Such was the situation that took us down the M6 past Cumbria and back to England, with so very much of Scotland still to discover. Years later we have still spent only a fraction of the time that we would have liked to in Scotland.

Chapter 6

TRAFFIC JAM

With no definite destination in mind we had decided to get past Carlisle and continue south on the M6, throwing ideas and suggestions at one another as we went. The golden sunshine of a May evening flooding through our windscreen, the old place had somehow defied all the odds and improved its weather. After thirty odd years of clouds and rain I was gaining a newfound respect for the sarcasm in its sense of humour. Eventually my darling mentioned Weston Super-mare, and, for no other reason than my liking the sound of the place, I agreed.

We never drive anywhere quickly, fuel consumption being most economical at about fifty or fifty five miles per hour, and with one or two stops for mealtimes included we had expected to arrive at our destination in darkness. Intending to find somewhere suitable to pull over and park up, it is often a good idea to wait until darkness has fallen. Only then can you see just how quiet a potential parking place really is. The matter was taken out of our hands though, traffic grinding to a complete halt shortly after we had passed Warrington.

At first we thought that we would begin moving in a short while. Most of the lorry drivers kept their engines running for a while, probably to keep warm, until they got sick of using their employer's money to burn a hole in the ozone layer and turned them off. At one point I almost began to feel sorry for the average motorist, even the women were disappearing into the bushes to answer the call of nature.

It was while we were sat there feeling a bit smug with the fact we not only had a kettle and a fridge but also a toilet, that I suggested we name the van. We bounced a few different suggestions back and forth between ourselves and at last settled on the name of

"Betty". After a while it became clear we were not going to move far any time soon and I told my darling to go and have a sleep on the sofa, while I sat in the cab on the look- out for signs of motion further up. Being careful to make as little noise as possible I spun the passenger's seat into a position which would allow me to put my feet up, and immersed myself in a book I was reading at the time.

A couple of chapters later I was in need of refreshment. Again being careful to make as little noise as possible, I went to the back of the van to brew a cup of tea and found myself under the watchful gaze of some no doubt very thirsty motorists. I'm not an uncharitable type of person but decided to close the blind without delay, in fear of people forming a queue to use our toilet. For a brief moment I was tempted to go and speak to one of them, in the hope of gleaning information as to what had happened. Realising my kettle would only boil enough water for a few cups at a time I decided against the idea.

Almost five hours later, I at last noticed movement up ahead, about four thirty in the morning. Unceremoniously I woke the little darling from her slumber, and somehow managed to stifle a laugh as she climbed behind the wheel not really knowing where she was. The queue in front of us gradually started to move and we worked our way up to our usual fifty five miles per hour, at which point I decided it was my turn for some sleep and reclined my armchair right back as far as it would go. I woke some time later to find the dear girl was motoring along at almost eighty miles per hour, as she often does when I'm not awake to reprimand her.

It was now my turn to be slightly disorientated. She quickly informed me that the stretch of water I could see to our right was the Bristol Channel, and I felt a wave of relief that this leg of our journey was almost over, as we seemed to have left Scotland an eternity ago. No sooner had we passed the Severn Bridge than the sun came up over the distant hills to our left. I'm not trying to say the M5 is a good vantage point for such a view, but experiences like this have taught me England really is a green and pleasant land from all sorts of angles if you give it a chance.

Arriving in Weston Super Mare we let the road-signs shepherd us directly to the beach, the entrance to which was guarded by an attendant wearing the obligatory high visibility jacket. The now radiant sun beaming down from a clear blue sky meant that there were no shortage of people milling around taking advantage of what was becoming a fine day, and the amount of cars parked on the beach bore testament to this.

I opened my window as we drew level with the high visibility jacket and a woman's face appeared, peering into the side of the van. Being that we are left hand drive I am sat on the right side of the van, and therefore used to people staring at me and wondering how I manage to drive from such a relaxed position, leaning back in the armchair as I usually do. I handed over the three pounds that the rosy cheeked woman requested and we made our way onto the sand.

Looking back I find this to have been one of the most reckless things we have done with the van. We took reassurance at the time from the fact that there were so many cars parked up on the beach, no doubt wondering what could possibly go wrong. With hindsight everything turned out ok and we never got stuck, but in truth I look back now and shudder at the thought of what might have happened.

We drove past the rows of parked cars and made our way to an empty section of the beach, the sand being firm beneath us and causing no problems at all. Away from the prying eyes of other beach goers, I soon had my weight training equipment out from the back of the storage box where it had languished pretty much unused since we set off from Cumbria. I thoroughly enjoyed my first workout in weeks, followed by a yoghurt and strawberry smoothy lovingly prepared by my darling.

With a daily newspaper to peruse I took up my place in the deckchair adjacent to that of my darling. Happily sat reading a novel, she now seemed fully recovered from the trauma of last night's slightly stranger than usual journey. With the golden sand stretching into the distance as far as the eye could see I considered us to have chosen the correct parking space. At such a safe distance from other people the only soundtrack to the afternoon was the crashing of the equally distant waves.

The three pounds we had paid to get the van onto the beach also entitled us to park on the promenade for as long as we chose, at least until the next morning unless the traffic warden worked nights. Needless to say my darling, who always has to have value for money, recommended that we also spend the night there, and so Weston Super Mare's promenade has to be added to the numerous places where we have watched Desperate Housewives.

On the way back from the shop with a newspaper the next morning, I received a text message from an old work colleague, to say that he was going to Huddersfield to start a new job. After a quick phone call I had arranged to go and start at the same job the following Monday, in about a week's time. I told my dearest the good news and she decided to throw caution to the wind concerning our remaining funds, taking me on a mini tour of the south of England.

Chapter 7

LANDS END

Our first night in Cornwall we spent on a camp site near Hayle. Unfortunately the good weather we had experienced earlier had not seen fit to accompany us into Cornwall as yet, and so I got rather wet as I rode my push bike down into the village in search of a second hand book shop. I was dismayed to find when I got there, that the only shop of such description they had, had closed some months earlier. Being quite a fan of real ale I consoled myself with a pint of "Tinner's" in one of the local establishments. As the name suggests, this is a brew which is local to the area, and is, I can say, extremely tasty. Whenever I am in a new area I always make a point of sampling the local brew, and Cornwall has never left me disappointed.

Watching the news and weather forecast later that night, my darling pointed out that we had rather cleverly managed to choose as a destination, the only part of the country in which it was raining. Therefore the next day we thought we would try our luck further towards Land's end and so made our way to Redruth. When I have mentioned this to anyone who knows Cornwall, I have often been met with a look of something approaching shock and horror. I can only assume that they think this a rather poor choice for someone with the whole of Cornwall to choose from. At this point I must point out though, before I alienate any readers who might be Cornish, that we enjoyed our stay in Redruth probably more than anywhere else in Cornwall.

We arrived there completely by chance. Probably because my attempts to take us to one of the typical camp sites you find in magazines, where the sun always shines and someone is out frying bacon on a barbecue, had managed to take us to the only place for miles around which had seen any rain of late, and so the responsibility of choosing destinations had been removed from my shoulders. Sometimes chance can be kind though, and on this occasion, this was very much the case. When we arrived we found a small car park, almost immediately, which had a sign reading "free until further notice", which to us was just too much of a temptation. Without any hesitation we parked the van and, as the weather had improved somewhat remarkably, set off walking into Redruth just a short way further down the hill.

No doubt remembering how wet and downtrodden I had seemed the previous day, returning after my abject failure to find a bookshop, soaked to the bone albeit semi-consoled with real ale, my darling pointed to a sign which indicated there was one down a side alley of the main street. At first there seemed only to be a limited number of books in stock on premises which were quite restricted to say the least. Further inspection, however, revealed a small doorway nestled at the back of the room, so I told my dearest where I was headed and set off.

In true lion, witch and wardrobe style this small door led almost to another dimension, first along a corridor lined with books and then into an area about the size of the local library back in Whitehaven where I grew up. I had browsed only a short while when I was followed by my better half, as she did so the same look of surprise developing on her face as what I must have worn myself a few moments earlier. A couple of hours later we emerged back into the real world, and as we now had books to carry back up the hill, decided to stop off at the pub for a refreshing pint of ole peculiar on the way.

We spent the whole of the next day sat reading our new books, in the aforementioned dodgiest free car park in Cornwall. In our defence the incessant rain had returned, and anyway we had decided to set off on the road to Land's End the following morning. Fortune was with us again, in that as we had decided to arrive "out of hours" as it were, we managed to park the van for free once again. Never being the sort to let our reluctance to part with cash stop us from doing things, we had a walk around without actually paying to go in and see. As the saying goes, the best things in life are free, and the views from Land's End visitors centre car park are no exception.

From Land's End we had a very difficult journey ahead of us, our next destination being the Minack Theatre, a place my more cultured better half had always wanted to visit. By now the road had deteriorated to a single track lane in most places meaning we had to round the corners with trepidation, in fear of a vehicle hurtling in the opposite direction. The van rolled to a halt in Porthcurno bay and we considered spending the night there, such was the tranquillity. In the end, however, it proved too quiet even for us. We settled on using the pushbikes to make the last leg of the journey to the Minack Theatre, again pacifying ourselves with a view from a distance as it was out of hours.

On the whole I found myself very impressed with Cornwall. Among other places we visited were Padstow and Newquay, both of which are worth seeing. Newquay, however, does have a lot of no camper van signs in its car-parks, probably due to the amount of surfers etc. who I assume descend upon the place in great numbers when the weather permits such pass times. For this reason I would certainly have a campsite booked in advance if I were to return.

Padstow in particular I found to be a very beautiful place, with a good number of public houses surrounding a very scenic harbour side. Unfortunately though, Cornwall had to be added to the list of places which we must return to, as the time we had there simply was not long enough. We have returned on numerous occasions over the years but always find ourselves in the position that we were that first time we visited, in that we are drawn away due to work commitments before we have managed to do even a small portion of the things which we intended on our way down the A30.

I hope I don't sound like someone who just wants everything for free when I tell you about our next destination. However, that is the way that things turned out through no direct fault of our own. Driving out of Cornwall on a fine morning in May, my darling was in such a good mood that she decided to rescind her earlier decision and allow me to choose our next destination. Having always wanted to visit the site of the famous battle in 1066, I was now presented with an opportunity to do so, and plotted a route which would take us along the south coast of England before she could change her mind.

Chapter 8

BATTLE

As most people will no doubt be aware however, the supposed site of the battle I refer to is not actually in Hastings but in the nearby and rather aptly named town of Battle. Unabashed by the bemused look that came across the face of the passing pedestrian I had asked for directions to the castle, I thanked him for this advice and bade him good day. During this brief detour we saw a sizable chunk of Hastings.

We had spent the previous night on a cl not too far outside of Hastings. With yet another navigational error under my belt the short journey we would have had, had become a little more difficult. My dearest was by no means in a fantastic mood when we eventually found Battle abbey and discovered that the car park was not exactly welcoming to even the smaller variety of motorhome. Due in no small part to her by now fantastic ability behind the wheel, we were soon parked up and having a quick bite to eat before going in search of what the abbey had to offer us.

A hundred or so paces later we arrived at a large double door, set back into the ancient stonework of the abbey. In the absence of any obvious alternative, I assumed this to be the main entrance. The security guard on duty was preoccupied talking to someone through the window of a car which had just pulled in, giving us only the briefest of glances. Eye contact had been made though, and if payment was required I presumed it would have been requested.

Emerging through the inner side of the arch we were confronted with the sight of that part of the abbey which now serves as a school. A few groups of pupils were wandering around, no doubt going from one lesson to another, all of them dressed in the same sort of finery not seen in the average public school for at least a hundred years or so. The sun had been shining brightly all morning, and although it showed no signs of abating we elected to walk the grounds before going inside.

The twittering of birds provided a soundtrack altogether different from how things must have sounded on that October day almost a thousand years ago, when the place had earned its name. As such the conditions were perfect for a stroll, and we climbed the hill towards the older part of the abbey feeling that we could have walked further. Along the way we had passed numerous small noticeboards, displaying illustrations and text giving us snippets of information relevant to certain parts of the grounds. By the time we reached the spot where, supposedly, the last Saxon king of England met his grisly end, I had begun to harbour a suspicion that we had walked the route in the reverse direction to that intended.

Indeed my suspicions were proved correct as we left the museum and gift shop, the latter having a reception desk where we would have been invited to pay an entrance fee on our arrival. On our way out of what we had thought to be the exit, I could see that from the outside it was clearly marked as the entrance. We were now only a short distance further along the street from the large double doors which had so fortuitously opened for us at the exact moment we were about to arrive, leading us to think they were the main entrance.

In our defence, we had hardly sneaked past the security guard. Indeed, if he had been observing the entrance to the car park, he would have witnessed us spending twenty minutes doing a ninety six point turn in order to gain entry. It's difficult to go anywhere discreetly with three and a half tonnes of motorhome. Anyway, seeking full value for the money she hadn't paid, my darling decided we were spending the night in the car park.

The next day we were out of bed early in case the abbey was inundated with visitors. It's always better to leave in a dignified manner of one's own accord, than to have some poor parking attendant confronted with the task of knocking you out of bed. A short drive later we arrived at Leeds castle where the parking situation could not have been more different from our experience at battle abbey. In saying this it is not my intention to be unkind to battle abbey. On the contrary I have great interest in anything of historical importance to our beloved country, and can only say that it is well worth a visit no matter whether you pay to get in or find yourself herded through the gate free of charge as we did. The fact remains however that the parking facilities at Leeds castle are far superior.

Having been ushered into our parking space by a parking attendant we left the van in acres of space and set off towards the main attraction. Even though it was by now raining ever so slightly, really just a faint drizzle, we refused the land train type contraption and opted instead for the walk to the castle itself. And very glad we were indeed that we had done so, the garden being so outstanding in its beauty that the magic had not been at all lost even after walking almost a mile from where we had parked the van to where we could enter the castle.

Our patience did however begin to wear thin when we at last got inside and found that we had managed to arrive at precisely the same moment as a large party of school children. Never one to be daunted by such turns of misfortune, I resorted to making the best of things, whilst quietly hoping that a suit of armour might come to life and start swinging an axe in the general direction of this travesty to peace and quiet, or at the very least fall rather unforgivingly on top of one of them.

Thankfully the rain had ceased by the time we came back out, and so after briefly returning to the van for dinner we decided to go back inside the castle and do the whole thing again while our tickets were still valid. The gardens were no less magical even by now, the morning's rain seemingly having done something to the colouring of the flowers. While I must admit to not knowing the name of a single one, even I found there appearance somewhat remarkable.

Of more interest to myself were the numerous large and apparently very old trees, and also the small stream which winds its way alongside you as you walk. We had now walked the full length of the garden four times in total and were still pleased not to have taken the soft option of using the land train. By the time we did finally return to the van my feet were beginning to ache though, and I enjoyed a very welcome cup of tea before we set off on the road again.

At this time we were not yet members of the National Trust. This is perhaps why we were so determined to return to the castle in the afternoon, to get our money's worth from our tickets having paid thirteen pounds each for them. If a similar situation were to arise at a National Trust property we would probably be happy to bid a hasty retreat and try again on another occasion.

 One disadvantage with the Trust, however, is that you always feel compelled to go to the nearest Trust property instead of following where your heart would instinctively take you. Perhaps because you are getting such a great deal in being able to visit free of charge once you have a full membership, I for one feel like I should not miss any that are even remotely close by. For anyone thinking of doing even a small amount of travelling around our country, I can only say that membership of the trust is an absolute must. Although neither of the properties I have just mentioned are Trust properties, there are many of similar quality scattered throughout England that are.

Chapter 9

BACK TO WORK

My darling has often quoted an old saying to me which goes something along the lines of visiting everywhere you go at least twice. Whilst we both remain largely sceptical I must admit that in early 2005 this certainly became the case for us. Having been in touch with my old friend and work colleague, and arranged to go to Huddersfield to do some work, we now made this our next destination. I had expected to recognise a few landmarks as Huddersfield is not exactly a metropolis, but I was quite taken aback when I realised how close we had been on our most recent visit, to a place which was now going to become home for at least the next few months. Indeed the very golf course we had sat next to eating chips seemingly an eternity ago, whilst on our quest to find the perfect vehicle, became the next place we parked while looking for a camp site.

At that time however we had no means of carrying a scooter, and so were limited to the push bikes for transport. Because of this I needed to be much closer to where I was going to be working than I do now. We managed to find quite a few camp-sites which were more than satisfactory. The trouble was that the place I was going to be working, a place called the Titanic mill on account of not only its size but also the year it was built, was in the middle of a somewhat deep valley. I would therefore, in the evenings, have needed to make an uphill climb on the pushbike of Olympic proportions. After a hard day this was going to be quite unworkable, and so we had to come up with another idea.

We drove a couple of miles further on from the Titanic and found the next village to be a place called Slaithwaite, known as Slawi to its inhabitants. This is a very old fashioned type of village with lots of terraced houses, but also with more shops than I had expected a village of this size to have. In fact although "Slawi" was little more than a bus stop it actually had a library, a launderette, numerous hardware shops, a gym, a fire station, various eating and drinking establishments and also a canal running through the middle upon which there was a floating tea room.

Alongside this floating tea room we decided to park. I would like to tell you that over the coming months I spent many a happy hour in this tea room, which was actually a converted barge. Sadly though, this was not the case as I had far too much work to do. Whenever we did get time off we wanted a change of scenery and would drive out of Huddersfield at the earliest opportunity, usually at about two o'clock on a Thursday afternoon if there were any way this was possible.

As things turned out we spent only a short time parked next to the canal, there were far too many people passing by for this to be an attractive long term option. Having noticed that the local conservative club had a reasonably sized car-park, I made it my business to call in for a pint and enquire about the possibility of becoming a short term resident. As luck would have it, the lady behind the bar that night was actually in charge, and so very kindly agreed to let me park up for the princely sum of ten pounds per week. So as long as I had full leisure batteries and a full tank of water before returning here on Sunday night I could last until the next weekend. The nearest thing to a drawback being the brass band that rehearsed on the premises every Wednesday night.

As my workmate was driving all the way back to Cumbria every weekend he liked to finish as early as possible. In his opinion, however, this gave him the right to set off at two o'clock on Thursday afternoon. As we were both self-employed this was of no great importance to anyone but ourselves as long as the correct amount of work was getting done, and so consequently most weekends for us began at about this time. I have many fond memories of driving through Huddersfield, en-route to our destination of choice, with all the windows open and the blowers on cool as we had many fine weekends that year. Sometimes we would travel as far as East Anglia in order to try out a specific camp-site which we had researched during the week.

One such site was a certificated location in Bungay, which only a few years previously had won an award for being "CL of the year". The standards there were still very high even though by now the elderly couple who ran the site were both of quite an advanced age. The place was just off a very quiet little cul-de-sac, something which in itself is quite rare nowadays. Upon driving through the gate the lucky visitor finds themselves in a very well kept garden surrounded by a circle of privacy giving trees, which also provide welcome shade from the sun on a hot day such as the one we were lucky enough to visit on. Since discovering this particular little gem I have harboured desires of my own for running such an enterprise in my own twilight years, so idyllic it was made to look.

On the whole though, we tended to stay a bit closer to Huddersfield, as there were quite a few places of note worth seeing nearby. Indeed we came to know the area surrounding Huddersfield in such a way that would never have been possible with any other arrangement (for example if we were staying in rented accommodation or if I was driving back up to Cumbria every weekend like my work-mate). It was around this time that we first became acquainted with Holmfirth, the very scenic and beautiful countryside made famous by the television program "last of the summer wine". Prior to now we had only ever been day visitors to this area on the extremely rare occasion we had enough time off work for it to be worth driving down. Now all of a sudden we were residents here and had what seemed like all the time in the world to explore at our leisure.

Of course we were not residents though. Appeasing ourselves to our situation, we had one last walk along the canal. By now it was late September and on this particular day the weather was nothing short of fantastic, as late September sunshine can often seem. All good things must come to an end at some point, no matter how permanent they may once have seemed to be. I truly believe that there is no such thing as a job for life in this world in which we live today. It was now three months since we had arrived, and as we headed towards Marsden the next village along, I think we were both saying goodbye to a place we had actually begun to like.

We did not know it at the time, but it was often to be the case that the places to which we headed for work reasons were the places which left the most lasting impression on us. Three months being, I think, the perfect amount of time to spend somewhere before it starts to feel monotonous. Perfect really, as ninety days is the amount of time required to receive a long term discount at many Spanish camp sites.

Chapter 10

ESPANA POR FAVOR

One of the many subjects we discussed at length, when first planning to buy a motorhome, was the idea of taking prolonged excursions to Spain. When we eventually arrived in Spain, however, it was with the minimum of organization, a habit which was becoming something of a trait. I look back in amazement at how we managed. We had sailed across on," The Pride of Bilbao" from Portsmouth, a crossing which at that time took two days. I remember it as being quite a pleasant experience on the boat, even having a couple of pints while my darling made use of the on-board hairdressers. We had boarded the ferry in Portsmouth on Christmas Eve and arrived in Bilbao on Boxing Day morning at around seven o'clock.

Soon after leaving Bilbao we pulled over and parked in a petrol station car park with the intention of booking a pitch somewhere. I shudder to think of how close things actually came to going wrong, as I realised when I started looking through our book of campsites that this was really something we should have done in the UK, especially as we'd had ample time to plan ahead having looked forward to this for such a long time now. Be it due to the fact the stars were correctly aligned or the wind was blowing in the particular direction we required I don't know, but somehow the first place we rang turned out to be the place we decided to head to, a place called La Marina which is on the eastern coast of Spain just past Benidorm. The main selling point of which had been the fact they had a gym which was included in the price of the pitch.

We had a long way to go as we were only just outside of Bilbao. This being the days before sat-nav (ok so it was available at a price but we never had one at that time) we had decided to go through Zaragoza and towards Barcelona before following the coast right down, rather than take the more direct route through Madrid. In no time at all we were on the toll roads.

The needle of our speedometer was hovering at an unusually clockwise angle, but knowing that we needed to be at the site for ten pm to book in I kept my mouth firmly shut, guilty of the oversight which had seen us arrive in a foreign country with so little planning. We arrived on site at about five to ten, although it would not have mattered if we were late as we could easily have spent the night in the late arrivals area, as we have done since.

The very kind reception staff, who thankfully spoke English as so many of the Spanish do, did not mind being a few minutes late going home, and booked us in without further ado. By eleven o'clock we were tucked up in bed completely tired out after a journey of epic proportions, having stopped only briefly for something to eat a couple of times on the way down. By nine o'clock in the morning of the first day after Boxing Day, I was stood outside the gym waiting for it to open, eagerly anticipating my first Spanish workout.

Over the course of the next few days I did what my darling calls my "hunter gatherer" part and we now had somewhere to go to by all the essentials, as the shop on site was quite pricey. As a rule of thumb I have usually found this to almost always be the case with on-site shops, although to be fair most people are just glad it is there for everyday things like milk and bread.

One other thing I always get from there is marmalade, something which the Spanish don't seem overly keen on. Their shops always sell apricot jam or even peach but very rarely marmalade, which I find particularly surprising given the prolific rate at which they grow oranges. In la Marina however they sell a particular type of marmalade which contains Cointreau, and having always been fond of whisky- marmalade I was only to keen to give this a try. I have loved it ever since and always bring some back to the UK with me. This is, however, the only place in Spain I have ever seen it on sale.

The current trend on European campsites is that they have a large satellite dish and run an underground wire to a bollard on each pitch, so that those who are so inclined can see what they would've been watching if they were still back home. Of course, I watch it myself on the odd occasion. At that time, however, there was no such luxury. My dearest and I have always remarked that the lack of it improved the stay, as if somehow making the days last longer.

Many happy hours were spent in our armchairs reading book after book, a fantastic luxury for me as I am always too tired to read after work. Within a couple of days I think we both felt extremely "at home". The fact that, for the first time since purchase, we had now parked the van and did not have any intentions of moving it (her) for at least the next three months, played no small part in the extent to which we were both now relaxed.

Sometime during the first few days we decided to take a walk to the beach. I had been out earlier on the bike and discovered that it was only five hundred yards away. Setting off on foot together with my dearest we went through a turnstile at the lower end of the site, which took a path through the woods and then across the sand and down to the water's edge. To me the beach was like an impossibly sunny location from an American television program of the eighties.

Words just can't do it justice really, but I better try. It had a walk-able length of about six miles I would guess, between a small river at one end looking towards Santa Pola, and a somewhat larger river at the other end where the beach approaches the small

Spanish town of Guardamar Del Segura. Somewhere in the middle there is a restaurant called bar Candela and also a nudist beach. While we are there the beach is not very busy except for the occasional couple or dog walker, usually fully clothed apart from one or two strange cases. Whether or not this is the case in summer I do not know.

Motorhomes are to be found in abundance along this beach, where access to and from the road allows. They tend to cluster in large groups probably for the sake of safety in numbers. At first we were quite surprised to see so many. Near the bar which goes by the name of "Bar Candela", there must have been at least a hundred of them. And so we passed quite a pleasant half hour looking at all the different makes and models whilst trying to spot any number plates with GB emblazoned on them, of which there were very few.

Having found it hard work walking along the sand, we soon discovered it better to walk right at the shoreline where the sand is still wet and so firmer underfoot. And so, to the shoreline we now returned in order to walk homewards back along the beach. By now the sun was past its highest point in the sky and no less pleasant for this, particularly when taken into account what the weather was no doubt doing back in England.

Strolling slowly back, we discussed the possibility of perhaps camping on the beach ourselves. The truth of the matter is though, that the main cost incurred is actually the ferry and the drive down. The thought of depriving ourselves of electricity and running water, not to mention the gym and the bar, did not seem worth the few hundred euros it would save us. Indeed, we found it quite puzzling that someone would pay so much for a vehicle and then skimp on the cost of a decent campsite. Besides which, neither of us could work out where they empty their chemical toilets.

It seemed like we had an eternity stretching in front of us, with which to do as we pleased. Three months was just too far into the future for either of us to worry about at the time. Having reached a nirvana of relaxation, we remained in this state of bliss throughout our stay.

Chapter 11

FOIVER A NOIGHT

Upon returning to the Uk we decided to try elsewhere for work, for no particular reason other than a change of surroundings really. To place this into context it must be remembered that this was early in 2006, and for most people of my age recession really was just a word which we had heard on the news in the early eighties but never really understood the meaning of. I look back now and wonder what we would have thought if we knew what turmoil was in the making. Like I say though, in 2006 this was the furthest thing from our minds and work in the construction industry was plentiful.

I have always found that a look in the yellow pages can yield dozens of local firms involved in my line of work. After which it is simply a case of calling round to see if they need labour. Another approach of mine is to go directly onto any building site we pass and ask the manager for the contact details of the relevant sub-contractor. After calling only a few of the numbers on our list, we struck lucky with a firm who were based in Birmingham and had arranged to go to a job in Malvern for the following Monday. Back in the van I had a quick cup of tea while we looked through our book of sites, and within the hour we were on our way.

Having a few days to spare before I was back at work we had reserved a pitch on what we thought sounded a nice site. It was situated in someone's back garden, being a certificated location. We drove through a very nice area to get there, and were soon parked up on the owner's driveway while he set about opening the electric gate that would permit us entry to the back garden. The house was by no means a mansion, just a normal semidetached nice looking property with a considerably large garden, also very well kept. The lawn was immaculate and although the owners obviously had neighbours, things were structured in such a way that it was very private. .

After such a long time off I was obviously dreading returning to work, and as is always the case this seemed to make the small amount of time we had left be over in a flash. Before I knew it we were getting out of bed for my last day of freedom, at least for the foreseeable future anyway. Being Sunday I nipped out to a conveniently placed shop which was not too far away, and bought our usual selection of Sunday papers.

When I returned my darling had a cafetiere of freshly ground coffee on the table and was just pulling our toasted brioche out of the oven. After a delightful breakfast, during which I consoled myself to my predicament with such lashings of my favourite cointrau marmalade that I was on the brink of inebriation, we settled down and spent the remainder of the day devouring that despicable waste of rainforest more commonly known as the Sunday papers.

The next morning we were out of bed early and on the road to an old school which was being converted into flats just outside of Malvern. Having been assured that there was an abundance of parking we thought that we might try our luck at sleeping on site in order to save a little money. That evening things were going well. I had gotten my first day over and done with, and we were settled down watching tv when there came a knock at the door. It turned out to be someone who was living in the former care-takers property who had nothing whatsoever to do with the construction side of the development, but was employed in some insignificant way by the company who were doing the developing.

He therefore had permission to live on site from someone considerably higher up the chain of command than my site manager. He was extremely polite and very friendly, even mentioning a pub down the road which I thought rather forward of him. I knew though that I had been talking to a jobs-worth, and sure enough the site manager told me the next day that I would have to move. This was a complete about turn, as he had been previously very happy for me to stay. I guess some people think they're too good to have neighbours, no matter how temporary.

Fortune was with us once more however, as we had only driven a few hundred yards round the corner when I spotted an American motorhome in front of a farmhouse. I quickly jumped out and opened the gate while my darling manouvered our beloved Betty onto the beginning of what was quite a long driveway up to the house. Being careful to remember to close the gate, I then set off walking up the drive towards the house. I am something of an experienced veteran now where farmyards are concerned, as I have stayed on many cl's which are actually part of a farm, but at that time this was not the case. Thinking to myself that the worst case scenario was the possibility I might be told to get off someone's land, I knocked on the door somewhat hesitantly.

I am by no means the most observant of people, and I have never been called nosy in my life. I do, however, remember thinking as I stood there waiting for a response, that if I had a house in such a state of disrepair I would most definitely have been living in the Winnebago which was parked outside. As I have said I was something of a newcomer to all things agricultural at the time. I have since come to the conclusion that the place was most likely very nice inside, as the guy obviously put warmth and comfort above outward appearances on the list of requirements after a hard day doing whatever farmers do. Quite a contrast to the busybody who made sure Betty was removed from where she slept the previous night, as he was living in a property he didn't own and no doubt doing very little for a living, probably whilst working for some sort of government housing agency.

When the door opened I was met by a rather dishevelled little chap who had obviously had a lifetime of hard work. I launched directly into my appeal for accommodation, stating that all I required was somewhere to park my van for a few nights each week, and had thought it worth asking because I saw he had a similar vehicle. I had been thinking that the use of a tap, along with somewhere to empty my chemical closet and perhaps an electric hook up, were not entirely necessary as I was intending to go elsewhere at weekends.

He gave me something of a quizzical look and simply said, and I quote " foiver a noight?" somehow turning the statement into a question which said if I wanted it enough I would therefore pay this gladly. This was not exactly cheap as many legitimate campsites were only charging four pounds a night at the time, and that was with showers and hook up included. He was prepared to offer a service I was in dire need of though and I accepted very gratefully, at which point he told me that I could use his tap and drainage. He even went on to say that an electric hook up would also be available at a small additional charge.

Feeling rather pleased with myself I made my way back down the driveway to share the good news with my darling. The only other condition placed upon us was that we must park alongside his Winnebago in an attempt not to arouse the suspicion of his neighbours. To us this was no problem at all, and soon Betty was quite happily sitting next to her new friend. In no time at all we were all set up with the telly on, having more freeview channels than we'd had in some time, and my darling was preparing supper.

In the coming weeks we only moved off a couple of times, as we had everything we needed where we were and could easily take a quick drive into Malvern for some shopping. Work was going pretty much without a hitch and the weeks were rolling by towards summer, which is always a relief to us as it means we can sit out under the awning in the evening and enjoy the odd glass of wine. As it was we had a good vantage point from which to see the comings and goings of life on a farm, which seemed to include a distinct lack of anything concerning farming.

The farmer had two sons for whom he didn't hesitate to ask me if I could find any employment, leaving the suggestion hanging in the air that he had no use for them whatsoever. I declined as politely as I could, by now being used to working alone. There was also a daughter of the family who drove a bright pink car and could often be seen wearing a boiler suit whilst wandering the fields with an air rifle, taking pot shots at anything that moved or indeed anything that offered no provocation whatsoever, no doubt in preparation for a somewhat unladylike career. Perhaps by now she is in charge of the place and the two boys must finally do what they are told.

From time to time the field would suddenly fill up with cattle or sheep and I would have to be rather careful on my way in and out. We were very lucky not to lose a window one afternoon when a large bull made its way between us and the Winnebago, thankfully it seemed to know when to turn its head so as to avoid impaling Betty with its horns. After that we made an effort to leave a larger gap between the two vehicles.

After about three months we were once again ready to move elsewhere, and as is so often the case this happened all of a sudden. I made my way back from work with all my tools and informed my darling of our situation, and within about fifteen minutes we were packed away and ready to hit the road, but first I had to go and pay our final weeks rent. I went round to the back door as I now knew this to be the best place to get a response. After a couple of moments wait one of the sons answered the door. Being in something of a hurry to go elsewhere I had no option other than to hand the money over, and I have often suspected that the old gent was led to believe I vanished without paying my last week's rent.

Chapter 12

THE MICROCOSM THAT IS SWINDON

April 2006 found us stopping at a certificated location in the small village of Swindon near Cheltenham, for no other reason than the price being only four pounds a night including electricity really. So once again Betty was sat in someone's back garden, although this time things were not quite so grand, but I suppose one can't expect too much at that price.

As is our usual habit we went for a walk around the neighbourhood after pitching up, the official objective being to find a local shop in order to buy the daily paper. It is probably nearer to the truth, though, for me to say that I like looking at nice neighbourhoods even though I would not want to swap predicaments with anyone. One of the justifications I put forth to friends and family when we discussed leaving the flat and buying a van, was that from a certain point of view we were just going on a really long house hunting expedition whilst living in a luxurious mobile accommodation unit, and I tell myself that this is true as we always have that as an option. Obviously we just haven't discovered anywhere that meets with mine and the little darlings rather high and exacting expectations.

The next day we were in need of a bit more shopping than could be sourced locally and so we made our way into Cheltenham in search of a supermarket with a reasonably sized car park. Usually in these circumstances we go in to the supermarket together and I will by a newspaper before making my way back to the van in order to "keep an eye on our home", which is really a way to escape trolley pushing duty. As we disembarked down Betty's steps I was greeted by the rather welcome sight of a large building site across the road.

I told my darling I would catch her up in the shop and quickly grabbed my hard hat from the storage box underneath the van, before making my way across and in search of the site office. In this age of health and safety I have learnt that it is always wise to wear the relevant equipment when going on to a site as a complete stranger and looking for work, as it is all too easy to upset the average site manager. My efforts were not in vain, and a few moments later I left the site with the contact details of the company in charge of sub-contracting for my line of work.

Back inside the van I took advantage of the peace and quiet that my darling's shopping expedition always affords me, to make a quick phone call. As expected I was asked to leave my details and told someone would get back to me, the receptionist never being in a position to say what work is available. Moments later my phone rang again and I was called upon to go into the supermarket to lend a hand with bagging up the shopping at the check-out.

We can manage to shop only once a fortnight if need be, as long as I can get milk and bread etc. as we need them. So with cupboards fit to burst once again we were once more ready to hit the road. The only thing lacking being some form of destination, as we had not decided where to go. The possibility that the phone might ring about potential work always changes things a bit, as we now didn't want to burn precious diesel going somewhere of our choice only to find we needed to be heading in the opposite direction entirely.

After a brief discussion and a look at the map we decided to go to Stonehenge having never been there before. No sooner had we turned onto the A303, which runs adjacent to Stonehenge, than the phone rang. I picked up right away and found myself talking to a guy called Matt, who asked me a few questions about the sort of work I do before telling me I could start on Monday. He then went on to give me details of the job and said he would meet me there on Monday morning in order to go over some paperwork.

It was only after I hung up and began to relay the details of the conversation to my darling that we both realised the coincidence, for we were now once again headed to Swindon. Not the small village on the outskirts of Cheltenham which we had left that morning, but the town of Swindon that is now more of a city in all but official status. As we passed Stonehenge I could not help myself feeling that we had been helped by the old stones in some way, or if perhaps the A303 runs along ley lines or suchlike. Whatever the truth I suspect mankind will never know the answer to this and many other such questions. What I do know for certain is that when work has been in short supply I have tried this again, and on more than a couple of occasions it has provided a repeat performance.

Our first night in Swindon we slept behind a petrol station next to a roundabout on the A419, commonly known as turnpike roundabout I think because the petrol station's address is turnpike road. If we had, by some miracle, picked up some sort of prosperous psychic energy from Stonehenge, then we certainly hadn't carried it along with us because the petrol station was closed within a few months and the roundabout had been bulldozed over in order to create a new road layout. No doubt the contractors who done the work would see things differently though.

Not too far away from where we stopped that first night there is a small bed and breakfast whose owners also run a small cl from there rather large garden. We came to know this well over the years, and still return there from time to time even now. The thing about Swindon, at least from our point of view, is that we have always found we are able to get whatever we are looking for there. Indeed there are two large motorhome showrooms yards away from what will, in my mind, always be called turnpike roundabout, even though there is no longer a roundabout there.

Work was going without a hitch, and most of the time we found it possible to camp on the building site. I have always found this preferable, as it enables me to work until long after everyone has gone home and probably still be showered and sat in front of the television before most of them. For instance if someone is driving for an hour in the morning to get to work and then an hour at night to get home, for a self-employed house builder such as myself this equates to two hours a day for which you are not only not being paid but you are also paying for your own fuel. Getting paid a price for the amount of work done means it is profitable for me to work long hours.

Take into account that I can work two hours longer and still be home sooner, with a very limited fuel bill and no council tax to pay, and you can probably understand why I find it better to keep my mouth firmly closed about the subject while I'm at work for fear of rubbing someone up the wrong way. To be fair most builders are concerned only with their own situation, and I have many good friends. One particularly good friend, although not a builder, we did meet in Swindon due to something of a work situation.

Having finished one contract, it was fortunate for us that the priory vale visitor centre was situated right on the edge of the estate I was now going to be working on. Intending to create a positive impression, the developers had decided against skimping on the visitor centre and so installed a large prefabricated unit, thereby eliminating the possibility of any dodgy construction work at the same time. It really isn't an exaggeration to say that no expense had been spared, as the term prefabricated unit did not do the thing the justice it deserved. They had even installed a nice gravel car park, which Betty had no hesitation in making her home.

I had less than a hundred yards walk to get to work from my front door and so I used to return home throughout the day for refreshments, a quick phone call ahead being all that was needed to ensure my dinner was ready and waiting for me on the table. On my second day there, however, it was my darling who rang me when I had been working for only an hour or so. The poor lass was in something of a quandary because someone had been knocking on the door and she had ignored it, big brave girl that she is. Without delay I set off walking back to the van, eager to see what the problem was and preparing for the worst. As I was so close by this must have been literally seconds after whoever it was had knocked on the door. I could see no one as I entered the car park and thought that the best course of action would be to go into the visitor centre, with the realisation dawning on me that I should have done this earlier.

There were other places we could probably park nearby so it was not the end of the world, but still it was with a heavy heart that I went inside to face the music. My anxiety was unwarranted as the lady turned out to be very nice, introducing herself as Jet. I explained that I was working on the building site across the road and my girlfriend was waiting inside the van for me. Apparently I had chosen a bad day to arrive as there was a meeting scheduled for ten o'clock, with people expected to begin arriving at any moment. Jet then went on to say that she would appreciate it if I could move but that I was welcome to return there the next day. Never one to let an opportunity go begging I took the chance to ask if it would be ok if we were to stay overnight, at which point I was told that would be fine and that my girlfriend must drop in for a coffee the next day.

When I relayed this to the darling it threw her into even more of a quandary, no doubt feeling somewhat foolish for not opening the door. On rare occasions I am capable of putting my foot down where the darling is concerned. Thankfully this was one of them, as I told her there was nothing else for it except to go in there the next day and explain. And so we met one of our best friends. Over the coming weeks I would often find that I came home for dinner and the darling was still sat in the visitor centre drinking coffee, and on more than the odd occasion I suspect something a little stronger. We had never had things so good in a long while and for a good three months I never walked more than a couple of hundred yards to get to work.

During this time we would spend all week on the visitor centre car park. By the time Friday night came round we would be out of water and need to charge the van's leisure batteries and so would often go to the cl at turnpike. Alternatively, if we felt like going further afield, my darling would have us a pitch booked elsewhere, usually somewhere in the Cotswolds as we were relatively new to the area and still exploring its many delights.

Chapter 13

STANDLAKE SHOWERS

As a result of the era of red tape, any building site manager who I approached about potentially parking my van on site would refuse instantly. Apparently this was because if anything did go wrong, for instance if someone was to break in and steal all the copper piping from a property as happens quite often, then the insurance company would say that the policy was void if anyone other than paid security had been on site overnight. As I thought about this the logic of the argument was glaring at me, and I began to realise that the way things were going I might have to find a slightly different way of doing things.

For the last few months though, things had been ok, I had been working in Brize Norton. The site manager and his assistant were both very easy going and had gotten to know me reasonably well. They were quite happy for me to move our van from one driveway to another as various different houses became complete, and so we had eventually made our way around the whole site sleeping on alternate driveways.

As the job came to an end I was still anticipating our next step whilst having no really solid ideas, except to say that whatever did happen I was determined to find another job that would enable us to continue living in Betty, even if that meant taking a pay cut. By now we were both well and truly in love with our new way of life, having been living in the van for over a year at this time. In construction, plans can change on a day to day basis possibly because very few projects ever seem to finish on time, and so I only found out our next destination for certain on the day I finished the last house I had been working in.

I was told to go to Standlake, a place I had never heard of at the time, but which will now be etched into my memory for eternity.

It is a small hamlet a few miles outside of Oxford which has two camp sites, one of which we had decided we were going to visit. I had just managed to squeeze the last of my tools into our outside storage boxes and climbed back into the van to find my darling still on the phone trying to get them to answer. With any other sort of business this would obviously be an extremely bad sign, but we know lots of camp site wardens who seem to think they are above answering the telephone, club sites being the worst of all. Many good sites are run by incompetent idiots and vice versa, so we decided to go there anyway as it was only a short distance from where we were.

Short drive or not I made a small mistake with the navigating and we seemed to be finding that the directions listed in the book did not quite tie in with what we saw when we entered Standlake. Basically everything seemed to be on the opposite side of the road from where we expected it to be. I had come to the conclusion that we must somehow have made our approach from a slightly different angle than the one intended, when I saw a sign directing us to a camp site. A wave of relief flooded over us as we made a left turn to follow the sign, and I put the map along with the book of directions to one side quite gladly.

After less than a hundred yards we saw another sign, this time instructing us to take a right turn but also informing us of the name of the camp site. Realising at this point that we had actually arrived at the other site from the one we had been trying to call, it was none the less too late as my darling had already made the turn. Slowing to the obligatory five mile an hour on site speed, we took a moment to observe our surroundings.

We were at the beginning of a short lane which was considerably wide and very well paved. A small wall, which had been designed to be slightly rustic in appearance, ran very neatly to our left hand side leading to a small layby in which arrivals were intended to pull to a halt. Right the way along the wall, the lane was lined with wrought iron street lamps, imitations of the type that would once have been powered by gas. Over the wall there was a playing field whose lawn almost made me want to buy a croquet set and start a new hobby, beyond which the field ran in to a copse of pine trees. To our right sat a log cabin, a sign outside proclaiming it to be the reception and shop.

A timeless moment had elapsed while we had been trying to take all this in, and we now both turned to one another and had the same wide eyed look that told us we were equally impressed. We got out of the cab chairs, and after a little pushing and shoving to sort out who was going first I followed her down the vans steps and across towards the log cabin. Dreading the possibility that there may not be a pitch available for us we stood at the desk and rang the small brass bell for attention.

As if by magic the site warden appeared almost instantly, with a happy and welcoming face. My darling always handles the pitch booking and as soon as I understood that we weren't being told there was no room at the inn, I wandered off around the log cabin to inspect the wares of the shop. Amidst the customary camping paraphernalia one could also buy essential food items along with things like ice cream, chocolate, crisps and daily papers.

What caught my attention most was a door at the back which led through to a small gym according to the plaque above the door. Also there were another two doors with pool one and pool two emblazoned across the top. Thinking that the cabin had surely been too small for even one pool I made my way back to the desk and stood looking at the fish in the aquarium while I listened to what the lady behind the counter had to say.

It turned out that my darling had got us booked in for the next week or so with a small discount, as is so often the effect she has on people.   Thinking that the warden had been talked into submission I looked to see if her face was still welcoming and was relieved to find this still to be the case.   It then transpired that there were indeed two swimming pools of a reasonable size which could be hired out and used privately for a small charge of twelve pounds per hour.   Each one having a hot tub along with a sauna and being completely private, we decided this was a bargain and made a booking for seven o'clock that evening.

Back in the van we had time only to convey to one another the feeling that we had landed on our feet once again, before she revved the van up and we went in search of our allocated pitch. At the end of the lane were two more of the old style gas lamps either side of a security barrier which opened electronically as we approached.   The rest of the site did not disappoint either, immaculately kept with flowers and shrubbery all over, pine trees surrounded the perimeter whilst the old fashioned wrought iron lamps which to me seemed completely magical were everywhere I looked.   There was no need to use our levelling blocks as the gravel pitch was perfectly level and within five minutes we were parked up. Having an appointment with a Jacuzzi and swimming pool in a couple of hours we limited ourselves to a light bite to eat, over which we had time to gather our thoughts.

It was only now we were beginning to realise how extremely fortuitous my discrepancy with the navigation had been. If we had went to the other site first, we would have just taken a pitch and made the best of things, needing to be in the area for work. Metaphorically speaking we would never have looked round the corner, the delights of Standlake thereby remaining hidden to us. To my knowledge this is the most fortunate error in navigation we have ever made, and we both agreed that the gods had well and truly been smiling down upon us.

At five minutes before seven o'clock we set off on the short walk back towards reception for our stint in the pool. Very often when pulling onto a new site the first thing we do is go and check out the shower block to see if things meet with our expectations, in this instance however it did not seem at all necessary as we could imagine the splendour without investigating further. Walking towards the log cabin we passed the sites own payphone which was inside one of the old red phone boxes that I think completely epitomises England, but is so seldom seen in our country now. Approaching the log cabin from a different angle, I could now see it to have been bigger than I had at first suspected.

Not being one to suffer heat gladly, due to my West Cumbrian upbringing, I spent only a couple of minutes in the sauna. Somewhat surprising as it may sound for someone who grew up in a harbour town, I can't swim either, and so walked right past the pool and proceeded directly to the hot tub in order to let the bubbles massage away the pain of the week's hard work. The little darling was doing her mermaid impression, swimming up and down the pool scarcely causing a ripple as if to make me feel even worse for my inability to do anything other than a mad splash in an attempt to stay afloat. I was quite happy to remain in the hot tub for the remainder of the hour, and so shouted across words to this affect. This set in motion the desired train of thought, and she came to join me immediately.

The following morning we had our ritual weekend breakfast, toasted brioche washed down with a couple of cups of freshly ground coffee. The sun was beginning to shine brightly in through the windows and it was obvious there was only the slightest of breezes, judging by the way the tops of the pine trees waved ever so gently against the backdrop of the clear blue sky. Thinking the day too good by far to waste, we set off out for a stroll.

After passing reception we turned to our right upon leaving the main entrance, and so walked further down the lane we had come along when looking for the site yesterday, heading towards the heart of Standlake and the village green. Almost all of the houses we passed were built out of traditional Cotswold stone, with window frames painted that particular shade of pale green which goes so well with such buildings. Add in the thatched roofs and the effect was completely idyllic.

Past the village green we turned off and walked down a smaller even quieter lane than the one we had just left, although prior to finding it I would not have believed this to have been possible. We were now heading out into the sticks as the saying goes, and consequently the houses gradually became larger and grander looking. One or two of them were bordering on mansion status, having huge stone gateposts complete with mythological looking creatures perched atop. One such place had a driveway so large we couldn't see the actual house, but could just make out in the distance that someone was working away in the garden using a blower to tidy up the leaves which had fallen from the trees.

Although we never tire of looking at such unaffordable properties, eventually our feet were telling us different and we turned around and headed for home. Thankfully I'd had the foresight to fetch a small amount of money with me, so as we returned we stopped off at a pub, very conveniently situated about twenty yards from the entrance to the camp site. Walking in through the door we were greeted by the sight of ancient timbers supporting the old ceiling, and shining horse brasses everywhere. At the bar I ordered a pint of Wadworth's real ale and a half pint for the darling, with which we disappeared into a quiet corner of the pub where the seating looked incredibly inviting, our walk having been longer than we both intended.

Chapter 14

EXTRA TRANSPORT

The transition from living in a flat and moving into a vehicle full time had been nothing short of completely magical, I would not hesitate to recommend the experience to anyone. The small problem of the health and safety boom stopping me from living on the building sites would be easily overcome, and with the addition of a scooter rack fitted to Bettys rear end we were about to have the means to carry another form of transport at all times. In order to afford this however, we would have to forego on our sojourn to Spain and winter was by now looming in front of us.

As usual when we have any motorhoming requirements, we purchased the most current issue of our favourite motorhome magazine, in order to look through the classified advertisements in the hope of finding someone competent. With the whole country to choose from this can still be a formidable task, particularly if you want something done at short notice as we always seem to. Eventually we chose a tow-bar specialist in Castleford near Pontefract, partly because the darling's father had recently moved to nearby Doncaster.

According to this advertisement they claimed to be able to construct their own stainless steel rack and fit it to the back of almost any motorhome, so I gave the bloke a ring and told him the make and model of our van. He seemed pretty confident the job could be done, but said he would need to have a look to be certain. He then went on to say that we were welcome to park on his premises overnight as other motorhomer's had done on many occasions before, even a power hook up being available. When he told me that the rack in question would easily be capable of carrying most 250cc motorcycles I had no more questions to ask and within twenty minutes we were all packed away and on the road to Castleford.

A quick look was all that the guy needed before saying that he could start the work the following morning, and that the whole thing would cost about eight hundred pounds. Feeling relieved that Betty hadn't fallen into the category to which the rack would not fit, we agreed immediately. Our timing had once again been perfect. It was now gone five o'clock, and as the workforce left the place almost became as silent as any of the cl's we're fond of, whilst obviously not being as visually endearing. Having plugged into the power hook up we closed all the blinds to hide the view, and at once we were at home again.

The next morning saw us wake at eight o'clock, and after a nice cooked breakfast we left Betty with the guy in charge and caught a taxi to a nearby shopping centre. I say shopping centre for I really do not know what name to give the place. It was one of those American style malls as they are called, and had its own cinema and the customary burger joint, as well as also having an indoor ski slope and seemingly hundreds of shops. Being something of a child at heart these places never fail to enchant me, especially with Christmas just around the corner as it was then. We had been told to pick the van up at about four o'clock, so with plenty of time to fill we headed straight for the cinema. Forever afterwards I will always be reminded of this day by the film "night at the museum" starring Ben Stiller.

Deciding to give the skiing a miss we opted instead for the less healthy but supposedly safer option of burger and chips, before making our way into the shops in search of a leather jacket to go with the scooter I planned to get. I am terrible at buying clothes and would no doubt have come back out looking like the Fonz, were it not for the fact the darling was overseeing matters. Without too much fuss we purchased a brown leather jacket to which I never gave even the remotest of glances upon entering the shop.

Soon it was almost four o'clock and we were both eager to be re-united with Betty. There is an anxiety that comes over us both when we leave the van with someone to get work done, no matter how competent they appear to be. So, feeling like we were collecting a relative from the hospital, we made our way back to the garage in a taxi. With relief everything had went according to plan and Betty was now the proud owner of a brand new scooter rack. The only thing lacking was the actual scooter, a problem we intended to rectify in the next few days. First of all we had to visit the darling's dad in Doncaster.

The darlings father moved elsewhere shortly afterwards and unfortunately we have never had reason to go back to the area since. For the purpose of the brief time we spent there, we booked into a certificated location. A reasonable distance from the main road, the (no longer working) farmhouse was idyllic in its silence. There were a couple of small fishponds and various water features dotted around in quite a tasteful manner, with the pitches being gravel and separated by enormous flower beds, all bordering onto a velvet like lawn. Best of all there was an old world type pub at the end of the lane whose ales I had every intention of sampling the following evening.

Having spent the greater part of the next day scouring through some magazines I had bought a few days previously, I now had a vague idea of the sort of bike I was looking for. Luckily, my driving license allows me to ride a 50cc motorcycle without taking any further tests or having to emblazon the thing with L plates, apparently if I had passed my driving test a year later this would not be the case. Therefore all I needed to do was go out and purchase a bike and get insurance. We decided to go to Shropshire as there was a cluster of dealers in the area who sold second hand scooters. By the time we met up with Paul for our evening meal in the pub down the lane, we had planned a route to Shropshire for the following morning.

By four o'clock the next day we had a little red moped fastened to the back of our van. The fastening had been the part I had actually been dreading, as we are always paranoid about securing things down before driving. I have a check list which I am compelled to go through at least twice before the van will go anywhere at all, and the thought of my having to secure this bike which must weigh at least a hundred kilos to the back of our beloved van, all while under the darlings watchful gaze, had begun to daunt me. I saw myself constantly being sent to the kitchen window to check there was still a moped there. In the end my apprehension had been completely uncalled for, I soon found that the bike goes on and off with ease and takes no longer than five minutes to be totally secured. From time to time though, I still get sent to the kitchen window to check it is still there, even today.

That night we drove straight down to Burford in the Cotswolds, to a little site we had come to love while I had been working in Carterton. It goes by the name of Wysdom, and although it is right next to a school it is strictly for adults only, a sought after retreat during school holidays. It is a very well kept camp site within walking distance of the beautiful town of Burford, and we go there as often as circumstances allow.

By the time we arrived there that night it had already been dark for a short while, so I took the scooter off the rack and left it next to the van on our pitch. The next day I rode up and down the lane a couple of times just to get my bearings, and found things much easier than expected. Basically you can't go wrong with a 50cc moped, you just turn the handle and it goes forward slowly. Or pull the brake and it stops. The thing won't go faster than forty miles an hour even going downhill with the wind behind it.

Having sacrificed our Christmas vacation to Spain in order to afford the scooter, we were both keen to hide ourselves away on a quiet site somewhere nice for what would be our first Christmas in the van in England. Unfortunately Wysdom was fully booked over the festive period, and had been for quite a while. The place I would absolutely love to spend Christmas at, Linkin farm park in Standlake which we had just recently left, closes down completely for a couple of months beginning in December. A fact which I always find completely bemusing, as in my opinion it would be the perfect venue for Christmas, especially if it happened to snow.

So with our two main choices ruled out we were now searching through our site directory's, in the vain hope of finding something my old foe, the greater spotted caravanner, had overlooked when planning their Christmas excursion way back in July or whatever they do. It really was beginning to appear that anywhere worth going to was already fully booked. This can be a problem when doing things at short notice, but sometimes for me there is no choice.

Eventually we found room at the inn, as the saying goes at that time of the year. The darling spotted a small classified advert in the back of the caravan and camping club site directory, an advert which I had no doubt flicked past without really looking at. On closer inspection though, it appeared really nice, having its own gym and a bar/restaurant. When the guy answered the phone and said that he had vacancies we were both over the moon as we were cutting things fine again, and would have to leave Wysdom within a couple of days.

Chapter 15

CHRISTMAS

Having made arrangements we were now looking forward to our first Christmas in the van spent in the UK. Obviously we would both have preferred to be in Spain, but at least there were small consolations like English television and beer, not to mention the fact I had a new toy in the form of a scooter fastened to the back of the van. So it was with high spirits that we left Wysdom touring park one bright morning in December, bidding the place a fond farewell as we always do, knowing that at some point we will return but knowing not when.

After a quick detour into Swindon, in order to use the Asda Wal-Mart we became so fond of during our time there, we now had every conceivable Christmas requirement squirreled away into one cupboard or another. Heading west on the m4 shortly before three o'clock it was still a moderately bright day, although cold and crisp. An hour or so later darkness had descended, with a thick dense fog following closely behind. By the time we circumnavigated Bridgwater and found our destination it was almost five o'clock. We had followed the route specified and found ourselves on a long and unlit road, which according to the given directions and some vague road signage would lead us into the camp site.

About a mile further, the road stopped winding and crossed a small bridge next to an old farmhouse and a huge willow tree. I recognised a small building beyond the farmhouse, which I knew from the directions to be the reception block, so we parked the van and I set off walking across, aware that it was almost five o'clock and the little office would no doubt soon be closing. The small bridge turned out to have been very tastefully constructed, and was there in order to cross a small man-made stream which came from the river and fed into a boating pond behind the reception block.

Unbeknown to me at that time the owner had actually farmed the land years ago, before getting into some difficulty or other and becoming fed up of the hardship. He then went and put a small sign next to the road, informing anyone who drove past that they could camp on his land, soon finding himself inundated with requests for pitches from people who had until then camped elsewhere in Somerset.

I opened the door to reception and stepped inside. Whilst being by no means plush or sumptuous, there was a feeling of a hotel reception about the place. A wooden counter ran from one wall to the other, cutting the room into two and providing a generous seating area for visitors, complete with some old leather benches and a radiator which was turned off. The customary brass bell sat on the counter, suggesting that if no one appeared I should ring for assistance.

I suspected my entrance had caused someone to stir from whatever they were doing, as the door closed behind me with quite a slam and I thought I heard an automatic buzzer which it must have triggered elsewhere in the building. Sure enough a door opened behind the counter and I was greeted by a quietly spoken man wearing a flat cap, seemingly he had come through from the adjoining farmhouse.

I told him that we had spoken earlier on the phone and that I was looking for the pitch he said he had available. He went through all the formalities in a brief but efficient manner, thankfully avoiding the pomp and ceremony that comes with entrance to a caravan club site, but also sadly lacking the warm personal touch of a cl owner. That's not to say that he wasn't friendly though, as soon as we spoke I decided I quite liked the guy anyway and booked enough nights camping to get us over the Christmas period and into the New Year.

Whether or not it was the fact that money had changed hands I will never know, but the old guy had opened up a bit and began to seem a bit more welcoming. We were still exchanging pleasantries when I realised what I must have subconsciously noticed as soon as I walked in, and so inquired about the lack of a Christmas tree. As the words left my mouth I immediately began to wish they hadn't, for it was now only a matter of days until Christmas and if he had any intention of decorating a tree to mark the occasion he would already have done so. Still displaying the amicable smile he wore when he came through the door from the farmhouse, he told me he was a jehova's witness and everything fell into place.

I thanked him profusely for the pitch and was about to bid him goodnight, then realised that he had stepped through a hatch in the counter and was putting on a coat. Feeling relieved that I had not caused any offence I followed him out into the cold December evening, waving to the darling to come with us as I tailed him around past the willow tree and into the site. He pointed out where everything was as we walked and I realised the place was bigger than I had thought, although with a distinct lack of campers as every pitch we passed was empty.

He told me that we could park on the tarmac opposite the shower block, behind which I could finally see a few shabby looking caravans. Feeling pleased that we were at least on hard-standing, I thanked him again and bade him goodnight. The darling had pulled into the designated space as we talked, so all I had to do was plug into the mains and get back in the van where it was warm.

Immediately upon my re-entering, we began to discuss what sort of place we had arrived at, and the degree to which it did not resemble the image conjured up by the advert. The darling had not yet noticed the few shabby caravans lurking behind the shower block, and was therefore in some distress that we appeared to be all alone. Looking through the window I could just make out some of the empty pitches with fog rolling across them, although the outside lights appeared to have been turned off in order to save money. We like quiet and solitude, but the whole place seemed to be eerily quiet. We had been told there was a pitch available for us, not that the whole site was abandoned and we could choose any of four hundred pitches.

I drew the darling's attention to the shabby caravans which were partially concealed on the other side of the shower block, and told her that at least we were not completely on our own. My news that we had managed to find what was probably the only campsite in England ran by Jehovah's witnesses, went considerably less than a small way to placating matters. Eventually we decided that the site must make good money during summer and the holiday season, to the extent that they feel little reason to make the effort in winter when things are always going to be quieter, and so close most of it down. After all it was a big place and must have at least three or four hundred pitches, cost incurring and unnecessary for the amount of trade available.

After some supper we settled down for the evening with the television on, me with a cup of tea in my hand. About half way through Coronation Street we saw the unmistakeable sight of approaching headlights as a motorhome pulled in a few spaces behind us, as if sent by the powers that be to allay our fears of the foggy and wintery night.

The next morning was the Eve of Christmas Eve, and we were out of bed for about nine, which is normal for us when I'm not at work. As I stood outside enjoying a post breakfast smoke, the guy who had pulled in behind us shortly afterwards came out, under the pretence of getting something from one of his outdoor storage lockers. We exchanged good mornings and I continued with my smoke, before noticing him coming across to talk to me.

He got right to the point in no time at all, inquiring if I intended to stay. I must have just looked at him in a quizzical manner, thinking he had overheard us talking about the misleading advert over our breakfast. It became obvious pretty quickly, however, that he was merely voicing his own opinion, an opinion he obviously felt quite strongly about, and which was causing him consternation.

He said he had booked a fortnight but would be leaving that day, asking for a refund of his money before he left, as things were not as he had expected. I could not help but wonder exactly what he had expected. Given that most people don't camp in winter, and those who do tend to stay inside their caravan, camp sites can be lonely places at that time of year, which is why many close for the festive period. In a half-hearted attempt to make him feel slightly better I agreed with everything he had to say, which wasn't difficult as he was pretty much right anyway. Intrigued now as to what had caused him to feel this way I decided it was time I had a look around the place in daylight.

My attention was drawn to the caravans hidden behind the shower block, as I felt that for some reason they had been hidden from view. They were located in such a way that, unless you were actually on one of those pitches you would have no reason to go there, and so remain more or less unaware of them. So as I finished my smoke I wandered around the corner and was met by a collection of about a dozen of the oldest and mankiest caravans I have ever set eyes upon, gathered in one place at least.

They all exhibited signs of life, cars here and there, washing lines strung about the place and awnings etc., but also the tell-tale signs that people were living here permanent were there in abundance. In one corner there was even a discarded fridge which had recently been used as a table, creating quite a contrast to the luxury campsite tantalisingly hinted at in the advertisement.

Next I went to find the gym and the restaurant/bar, for which I had noticed signs above doorways near to reception the previous night when I arrived. With only a small amount of dismay I found that the gym was closed until after Christmas, I had been intending to rest anyway and was only mildly disappointed. Of more immediate concern was the bar being closed, I had little intention of risking the food but a pint or two would have been nice. I now knew from the note on the door that it was closed until after the festivities, a strange choice at what is normally the busiest time of the year for anyone who sells alcohol.

Back in the van I relayed the details of my conversation with our fellow motorhomer to the darling, and reported my findings concerning the caravan scrap yard around the corner as well as the closed gym and restaurant. Like myself she was more or less indifferent to the situation, we even had a mini laughing fit as we watched our disgruntled neighbour unplug his van and drive off an hour or so later, no doubt having been told what his chances of a refund were. Nor could the subsequent discovery that the shower facilities were also considerably less than adequate take any of the wind from our sales, Christmas was upon us and we were both in high spirits.

For the second year running we had Christmas dinner in the van, the darling produced a culinary delight second to none, with turkey and all the traditional trimmings. The fog eventually dissipated leaving behind it the sort of withering cold found only in December and January. With our heating purring away nicely we spent many happy hours reading and watching television.

Chapter 16

RECESSION

Everything had been going well really. We went back to Swindon after Christmas, spending much of our time at turnpike road from where I could use the scooter to get to any number of sites, work still being plentiful as it was. In fact there was such an abundance of construction work available in Swindon in early 2007, that I found I had only to call any one of a dozen contractors and I would be told I could start within a couple of days. This led me to develop a strategy whereby I moved from one job to the next, and capitalised on the best which was available in my line of work. Being prepared to go to any area was a big advantage, in comparison to most builders who like to limit their fuel bill since it comes from their own pocket.

In the summer of 2007 work seemed to take us on a tour of sleepy English villages, along what is sometimes known as the M4 corridor, also introducing us to the delights of such places as Bath, Devizes and Oxford, whenever we so desired it. For the greater part of the year though, I kept my nose to the proverbial grindstone as it were, often working Saturdays and Sundays. We began to think of our jaunt down to Spain, in the frame of mind that we deserved it having missed the previous year. Then in September we had the northern rock fiasco, and the rest as they say is history.

We did actually manage to get to Spain that year. Christmas is always a bit slack in the house building industry, officially bricklayers are not allowed to lay bricks below a certain temperature and this has a knock on effect with the whole industry having a slightly quiet period throughout the depths of winter. With this in mind, and rather than spend a winter in the UK and out of work, we threw caution to the wind and headed back down to la marina. Having such fond memories of our previous visit it was an easy decision to make.

At that time, when we used to go to la marina international camp site, we had no means of receiving an English television signal as the process required a dish of some two metres in diameter. Bearing in mind that an English newspaper will cost two euros per day, it can be quite easy to become distant from the news. Only when we returned to England in April of 2008, did we begin to realise the full extent of the financial difficulties the world now faced, Spain seeming to have its own money problems perpetually.

In truth that is probably one of the best things about going, and i remember those days without television somewhat fondly if I'm to be perfectly honest. The darling and I would sit side by side in the sun reading all day, only to retreat into the van when nightfall descended and pick up where we left off after supper. On many occasions I have sat and read a full book in a day.

Having disembarked from the ferry at eight o'clock in the evening, I made a quick phone call to our friends at Turnpike in Swindon, in order to get permission to pull onto a pitch late into the night. We had arranged to have an M.O.T done on the van the following day in Swindon, knowing that the garage we would use is conveniently situated to our regular campsite in Turnpike.

That familiar feeling of leaving a relative at the hospital returned as we walked out of the garage to where our taxi was waiting. Having heard nothing from the garage by one o'clock, we removed our minds from the problem still further by settling down in a pub and ordering something to eat. Sure enough our efforts were rewarded, shortly after we had finished our dinner the phone rang. By two thirty we were reunited with our beloved Betty, who now had a renewed M.O.T.

Back in the van we headed straight to asda on priory vale, parking up with ease at the far end of their large car park. As the darling went inside to begin shopping, this time for food, I made myself a cup of tea. Sat outside on the step enjoying a smoke and drinking my tea, I noticed how cool the sun felt, now that we had moved a couple of thousand miles north. Considering it a blessed mercy that I could see it at all, the sight of some distant clouds approaching turned my thoughts toward the ominous matter of my imminent return to work. On impulse I reached inside my pocket for my mobile phone, finding out that it was now three o'clock in the process. Being a very good time of the day to reach him, I rang my most recent supplier of work.

It was with mixed optimism and pessimism that I made the call, for I had by now seen enough of the news to know that things were not good. As I had almost expected, my contact answered the phone and said he had no work for me. What surprised me though, was that he went on to tell me that he was no longer in business. Knowing that he had been in business for twenty five years, and just a few short months previously had been doing very well, I was quite taken aback.

Taken by surprise I could only think to ask him what had happened, knowing him also on a friendly basis, to which he responded by inquiring if I had been reading the papers. A paper was something I had been looking forward to anyway, so I opened the van door and pressed the switch to withdraw the step before locking up and following the darling into Asda.

Uttering profanities under my breath, as is my way when searching a large supermarket for someone who refuses to answer their mobile phone, I eventually found success in the women's clothing department. I then accepted full responsibility for the breakdown in communications on the, what I must admit were very logical, grounds that I should have looked there first.

Differences duly settled, and with me feeling completely in my place, we made our way round Asda with our trolley as it seemed to rapidly fill itself with all the things we had missed during our time in Spain. As we walked I relayed the details of my phone call and we discussed the possibility of looking elsewhere for work.

By the time we were back in the van with all the shopping put safely away, we had sort of decided to go to Peterborough, due to there being a large house building project there at least until recently. After consulting our caravan site guidebooks for just a few moments we now had a specific destination once again. The darling got herself comfortable in the driving seat, while I went through the customary checks that all was in place, and we set off on what was to be a difficult route consisting mainly of dual carriageways.

One arduous drive later we arrived at a site in Peterborough. Pulling onto a pitch after dark can be difficult when you have no previous knowledge of the camp site, but after having had plenty of practise, we now find we can do so with ease. Within minutes of arriving we were plugged into the mains and I had the telly tuned in, while the darling had dealt with the kettle and had a cup of tea waiting for me. Consequently it was not until the next day that we knew much about our surroundings, when we found that we had pulled into what was quite a nice site with large pitches all surrounded by huge trees.

The next morning, when I ventured into the small hut like structure which served as a reception, I found four people sat round a gas heater in the fashion familiar to campsite wardens all over the country. I informed them that I had arrived late the previous night, as arranged beforehand by a telephone call, and was made to feel welcome straight away. Open friendliness is by no means a regular occurrence with camp site wardens and the matter perplexed me somewhat, until the darling pointed out that they were volunteers who worked for a free pitch and so not club employees at all.

Although the sun was shining quite brightly, it was still rather a cold day. With this in mind I had donned a thick top underneath my leather jacket, in order to try and stay warm on the scooter. I found my way round Peterborough quite easily and had soon visited the offices of all the big developers. Most of them were pretty helpful, supplying me with phone numbers if I asked, but I was given a distinct feeling they had grown used to visitors looking for work like me. The trouble was that the whole industry seemed to have slowed to a virtual standstill, with unfinished projects now crawling at a snail's pace toward completion.

A scooter is not a warm place to be at the best of times, having been out for what seemed like ages I was grateful for the warmth of the van when I at last reached home. As expected the darling had dinner ready for me, and so with a full stomach I sat back in my armchair drinking a cup of tea. After leafing through my book of contacts I decided to make a last ditch effort to turn things around and rang every contact I had, eventually striking it lucky with a firm I had worked for before for a brief time.

It became clear to me that I was lucky to have the contact, for if I had called as a stranger I would have been told the by now familiar line of there being no work. Were it not that I discovered the joys of Swindon when I did, and was instead arriving now, I suspected that I would have found a situation not too dissimilar to the one I had seen in Peterborough that afternoon. As if being an omen of things to come, the first place to which work was about to take us was in our faithful old stomping ground of Swindon. Being that this would be the first work I had done in months, I felt relieved to be going somewhere I knew as I rang turnpike to request a pitch for the following Sunday night.

Over the course of the next few days we spent many hours walking in the woods behind the camp site, savouring our last moments of freedom. When we were due to leave on Sunday morning, I went back to the reception hut and found the four old codgers arranged in the same manner as before with the heater. Knowing them to be reasonable folk I obtained permission to leave our van on site until the afternoon, and the darling and I took the short walk to the pub at the end of the road exploiting the opportunity to sample their roast dinners.

Back at turnpike it almost began to feel like nothing had really changed, except for one of our neighbours having traded in their hymer on e-bay and come away with a large but considerably older American rv. Of no consequence to me except for the fact he kept telling me he," should've done it years ago" to the point where I began to dread the sight of him.

One other thing which my neighbour was quick to remonstrate about was the fact our pitch fees had increased since the last time we had stayed. As reported in the news families had been going camping in their droves, unable to afford the holidays abroad of yesteryear. As a direct result site owners had seen fit to capitalise and increased their fees accordingly.

It was clear to see, however, that there was not a lot of construction going on in the area. The bed and breakfast next to where we camped had always been fully booked, now it was always empty. In contrast to the hitherto unquestioned philosophy of lending more money than was necessary to almost anyone who asked, over the coming months the banks now adopted an altogether different policy of scarcely lending any money at all, thereby worsening an already dire situation.

Chapter 17

ROYAL VISITOR

Later that year, the summer of 2008, work had taken us to Oxford and we had been camped on a club site just outside the ancient city, from which I was able to reach my job in about five minutes on the scooter. As a rule the darling and I tend to stay away from cities, an exception having to be made for Oxford, on account of the amount of history there. During those few weeks we ventured into the city on only a handful of occasions, preferring instead to have a walk along the riverside if the weather allowed us to.

I have an aversion to anywhere there are a lot of people, but nevertheless we somehow managed to accumulate a lengthy list of things we had done. Along with the usual things people tend to do in Oxford, like a ride on an open top bus, we also endeavoured to see a good selection of the old colleges there. One day we even managed to fit in a visit to the old prison and a punt along the river.

When the inevitable happened, and the time came round that work once again dictated we must go elsewhere, we were pleased to be asked to go to a more rural location once again. This time I had been asked to go to a place called Overton, near Newbury and Andover. Everything had been arranged a few days in advance, and after a last walk along the river we set off to a farm cl just south of Newbury, our guide book having informed us it was only a few miles from where I would be working. I made a small error with the navigation and we came off the A34 a couple of junctions too early, proving to be a costly error in that it meant we had to drive through Newbury on Saturday afternoon.

Coping well with the sudden change of plan, the darling safely made her way through the town centre and back onto the road the guidebook instructed us to take. Having passed through the village of Kingsclere, neighbouring village Highclere later made famous by the television program, "Downton Abby", we then took a sharp left and began to climb a steep hill. Kingsclere being an old village with narrow roads I had hoped that we were past the most difficult part of the journey, but now we were heading up a steep incline on a single track road. In such circumstances one can only guess at how much more difficult things will become before the destination is reached, the fact we had unnecessarily driven through Newbury contributing to our fatigue.

The road levelled out for a short way and, slightly earlier than expected from the given directions, a turn off appeared to our right hand side. Thinking this had to be it we turned right, noticing our error almost immediately. Feeling like giving up I had to get out and check the road was clear for us to reverse. I climbed back in and we set off again undeterred, me apologising for my second navigational error as I got back in my seat.

Giving a rare blast on the horn, something only ever done at my insistence, we tentatively rounded a blind corner at the top of hill and at last the entrance to the farm was in front of us. Betty screeched with discontent at the overhanging branches, jutting from either side of the narrowest of lanes, before finally the darling brought her to a standstill outside of a small cottage. A quick check revealed there to have been no damage done to the paintwork, and we had maintained our record of managing to gain entry to any site we chose unscathed.

The cottage sat amidst a large garden which was well looked after, with trees marking the circumference and a small pond near to the front door. A couple of knocks on the door yielded no response so I headed further down the lane we had just come along, waving to the darling to rev up and follow me. We went through another small lane, though not as tight as before, which soon opened out to reveal two long fields stretching into the distance either side of a hedgerow. A few yards away from us the hedge opened out where a gate had been installed, providing a magnificent view across the green hillsides that rolled into the distance.

As if he had thought the scene needed to be more idyllic, an elderly gentleman I would come to know as Amos leaned farmer-like on the gate. A retired farmer he turned out to be, his son Joe seeming to do all the work with the patients of the proverbial saint. Having heard our approach he turned round to greet me, smiling broadly from his open and friendly face. I referred to my phone call a few days previously concerning a pitch, in response to which I was told where the electric hook up and tap were etc.

At that point my attention was drawn to whatever it was he had been looking at in the field behind the hedge, being that I could hear something going on but could not see down towards the bottom of the field. Noticing my curiosity he proceeded to tell me that he also had some industrial units he let out, one of these being occupied by someone who used it as a hangar from which to run a light aircraft repair business. The field behind the gate being the runway, I would often be able to see light aircraft coming and going, as they were at that moment. Anything sounding louder than this, he went on to say, would be the ministry of defence. Frequently they would use whichever part of his land they chose to practise landing Chinook helicopters.

Amos then told me of the various footpaths leading out of the adjoining field, the one in which I would be camped. A trail known as "the wayfarers walk", ran straight through the farm leading to Watership Down, made famous by Richard Adams in his book of the same name. I tried to hand over some money for the pitch but he waved my hand away saying, "berra let t' woif deal wi tha" in his heavy rural accent. Eager to share my opinion of our new surroundings I climbed back into the van, and we made the short drive down the field. After a slightly heated debate concerning exactly where we should park the van, I did exactly as I was directed and climbed back out, in order to await further instruction.

Duly parked the van window came down, and the order to place our levelling blocks in front of the wheels was given. I got them out of the rear outdoor storage box and at the first attempt the van was level. Without interference from me we now had a perfect pitch. We were facing the right way to make optimum use of the sun, free heat being gained from it hitting the windscreen. The tap was within hosepipe distance, meaning an easy job to fill the freshwater tank. When I returned to the cottage in order to pay for my pitch I met Annie, Amos's wife. I was given a fifty% discount on my pitch for the couple of weeks I had booked, Annie telling me that Amos had said to do so.

With the kettle on I started what is usually my next task after moving. I got our telly out from its hiding place and began a search for channels using the freeview receiver. We watched in a form of mild amazement as the channel counter went up and up. The most previously found by us at that time had been around fifty, back in the flat we had only ever found thirty or so. In the time it took to boil the kettle the thing had found in excess of ninety channels due to a television mast on an adjoining hill.

Over the coming months we spent many hours walking the footpaths that wound the hill in every direction. Going one way we could get to Watership Down within twenty minutes, a walk that provided magnificent views toward the horizon. Another favourite route of mine incorporated stopping off at the pub in the village at the very top of the hill, from where we could continue to other small villages if we so wished. The roads were pleasant to walk and very quiet, on many fine afternoons I would count more traffic in the sky, with light aircraft coming to use our neighbour's runway by the dozen if the conditions were right for flying.

A change of routine one Sunday led to us setting off out for a walk at about ten in the morning, as opposed to one in the afternoon when we would normally partake in such a venture. Deciding to take a different route we chanced upon four or five golf buggy type vehicles quite similar in design to the quad bikes commonly used by farmers. As they drew closer it became clear that the passenger of each vehicle had an arm held at an angle providing a perch for a large bird of prey. They stopped right next to us and disembarked from their buggies, and I could see that each bird appeared to be about twenty inches in height and was wearing a small hood.

Someone opened a gate in the hedgerow and the rest all filed past him and into the field. As they paced off across the field the man stood there leaning on the gate. I could see I was being given an opportunity to join them, and said good morning as a way of opening the conversation. I was told that for a small fee I could have breakfast at the farm before going out to watch the birds being used to hunt. I thanked him and said I would consider this, but could not resist watching from the road and taking pictures on my phone anyway.

From time to time the ministry of defence would arrive and the thunderous roar of Chinook helicopters would make the van vibrate when they passed what must have been mere feet above us. This was at the time when Prince William was training to be an air rescue pilot, and at a reputed fifteen grand an hour to keep a Chinook in the air, the country probably doesn't train many people per year to do this. When they first arrived we would take photographs and video footage, as they would often land in full view of us just a hundred metres away. It would be difficult to make a positive identification of someone wearing the full face helmet of a helicopter pilot at close quarters, never mind at that range.

Soon the novelty value of our visitors wore off and we were left only with the noise pollution. Then one evening there was an article on the six o'clock news saying that Prince William had landed a Chinook helicopter in a field belonging to Kate Middleton's parents. He was reported as having flown from Odiham air base, about twenty miles from where we camped. I was later to find out through the press that the field in question was in Bucklebury, about fifteen miles in the other direction. To this day I am sure we had a royal visitor on these frequent occasions, and if ever there is any value attached to video footage of a prince learning to fly a helicopter I must find a way of corroborating this story, for I still have the footage.

Chapter 18

THE APPLIANCE OF SCIENCE

From the perspective of anyone who does even a small amount of camping, things have changed quite dramatically in recent years. I am referring of course to certain technological advances made in recent times. For instance in the early nineties very few people had mobile phones, no doubt making wild camping an altogether different experience. Even when we first started there was not really an affordable way to have internet access in the van. Then along came the dongle in 2008, a small device containing a sim card, and all of a sudden this is a simple matter for anyone with a laptop.

The lack of a permanent postal address has never really caused us much concern. When necessary I find a post office that will let me use what is known as "post restante", whereby I can have mail delivered to their office and collect in person. There have been times however that I have found e-mails to be of particular use. Being free and delivered instantly, and classed as legal documents as they are nowadays, they are more use for invoices and payslips than letters or faxes ever were. Once we have something we often wonder how we managed without it, and for me this could not be truer than in the case of satellite navigation. I had always shunned the idea of it, considering myself an adequate map reader. Then after having had a little difficulty in finding our way past Newbury, I began to adopt a different viewpoint.

Having enjoyed our ritual Sunday breakfast of toasted brioche with marmalade and freshly ground coffee, we then turn our attention to the Sunday papers. Drawing articles to one another's attention as we find them, we have been known to spend the whole day in this pursuit if the weather dictates it so. It was on one such day that the darling gave me an article to read about smartphones, a particular brand now having satellite navigation as standard. We began to discuss the matter, as we had done sporadically in the past. The fear always having been that we might be led down an alley, as is often seen with eastern European lorry drivers, who must follow the device like it has some sort of divine power.

The obvious answer being, we decided, to not just blindly follow the thing but instead use it as an aid to my map reading. If nothing else it would have been useful on two occasions very recently, simply by telling us we were on the right road and not to turn off it. The recalling of a vivid memory of spending a couple of hours struggling to get out of Zaragoza while it was swarming with inebriated revellers on our most recent trip to Spain was all it took to convince us, and I went into Newbury later that week and got one. Right from the start the thing displayed a somewhat audacious talent for talking at the same time as the darling, showing scant regard for the number of times it was sworn at. Harmony was duly restored when I discovered a mute switch, and we now silence the thing when we know where we are.

There have been many other advances which make life easier for a camper, for instance many caravan owners have electric movers fitted next to the wheels of their caravan. The roller engages when required and moves the wheel in the desired direction, working on power from a leisure battery. Hopefully this may one day eliminate the sort of camper who comes rushing out of their own vehicle as soon as they see someone new pull onto site. You may think I am being harsh but spare a thought for the poor old couple who just want to get pitched up without interference. In my opinion, it is the equivalent of accosting someone in a hotel foyer as they are still carrying their luggage.

Until very recently, anyone wishing to take their favourite films along with them, or music for that matter, would have been very selective when choosing cumbersome cassettes or discs with which to clog up their van storage. Now a device the size of one cassette can hold thousands of films and music or even photos, and all of a sudden storage is no longer an issue. If we had to carry every photo I've taken since we got a digital camera, we would need a trailer. As for the quality of television reception, that has improved in leaps and bounds across the whole of the Uk. With the demise of the old analogue signal and the arrival of the digital era, having only four channels to choose from is a distant memory even for those like me without a satellite dish. In Spain we find now that a dish is completely unnecessary as there are aerial sockets on the pitch next to the power hook up, a few channels being provided for each language as would be found in a hotel.

One thing I never tire of seeing on campsites is the obscenely large Rv type vehicles, which I see in increasing numbers while in Spain though not so much in the Uk. Just a short while ago vehicles of that size were only built for the American market, whereas now there are two or three European manufacturers who have started to produce larger vehicles. Certain models even have the ability to carry a small car, in a garage fitted into the back beneath a fixed bed. Of course the money required to equip oneself to this standard is beyond most people. I can't help note, however, that in ten years such vehicles will be on sale second hand, and regardless of specification the price would have to reflect that it is a ten year old vehicle.

Certainly for anyone who drives alone without a co-pilot, I would say that sat- nav is a complete necessity rather than a luxury. For me it became invaluable straight away. Due to the unpredictable nature of the construction industry, from time to time I am often asked to go to a job at short notice. This might be because there is no work ready for me to start at my own site, or perhaps a site elsewhere might be shorthanded. Something like this can turn up every couple of months, or alternatively it might not happen for three or four months, the only certainty being that things never go to plan for long.

Upon being informed of such a situation in the past, usually by phone call while I am at work, I would have to write down directions dictated to me via the phone call. With the sat-nav installed on my smart phone all that is needed is a post code, then, with the phone in my pocket, I use an earpiece to listen to its voice commands while I'm on the scooter. Having disregarded the need to memorise and follow complex road signs in a strange place, I am then free to pay complete attention to the road and its other users.

Of course the first thing I will do is ring the darling, who will immediately begin a search for a campsite if required. On the rare occasions that our campsite guidebooks have let us down, needing to be in a specific area and not being able to find a site nearby, I have often resorted to searching google or google maps. The latter in particular can be extremely helpful, for it will search specifically the location of the map you are in or specify it to. Having arrived in a fresh pasture as it were, this can also be useful to find such necessities as newsagents, supermarkets and of course public houses.

As it turned out, when the call came to go to another job, we were being sent only a few miles down the road to Andover. I had been told I would be there for about three months, so we had booked a campsite in Stockbridge, where once again I would only be about five miles away from work. Thinking it very likely that we would be returning, we said farewell to Amos and Annie and headed first to Newbury, in order to use the supermarket we had become familiar with over the last couple of months. With the sat-nav chuntering away on the way down we had none of the difficulties experienced when I would navigate direct from the map, with u turns at roundabouts and reversing round corners a specialty, and after a rather pleasant drive we arrived in Stockbridge on a mildly autumnal Friday evening.

Our cl was just a mile outside Stockbridge, another farmyard site. This time we found ourselves in a field which was encircled completely by thick hedgerows, meaning nothing could be seen to either side. Liking the immediate feeling of the place we had a walk around after parking up. The club guidebook which had brought us to the site mentioned that the land behind was owned by the National Trust, and was very good for walking. We had no intention of walking very far, after having traipsed around a supermarket food was at the forefront of my mind.

When we found the opening at the back of the site it looked inviting in a magical kind of way, like something out of secret garden. The grass had been kept quite short and we could now see that a grassy path ran through the opening, bordered on either side by the hedgerow. Having been purposefully grown this way and tended to, the hedgerow at this point became more refined, like that seen in a garden.

Putting thoughts of our supper to one side for a brief moment, we walked along the path until ten yards later it split into two directions. One could be clearly seen running back to the farm, while the other ran in the opposite direction. Heading away from the farm we walked only a short way, until the track began to wind uphill, before we turned back. The hedges to either side of the path remained above head height for most of the way, opening out at one point and providing a magnificent view across the adjoining fields and towards a sun just about to set. Weary with hunger we decided to save the rest of the walk for another day, and retired to the van for refreshments.

We were to enjoy that walk many times over the coming weeks, while the weather remained amicable. To say the steep climb up the hill proved worthwhile would be an understatement of considerable magnitude. It turned out that there had once been an iron-age fort at the top, the views in every direction being magnificent. If we felt that we couldn't manage the climb up the hill we would walk down into the quaint town of Stockbridge.

The town of Stockbridge with its long and varied history has inspired many poets over the years and there is a trail of ten poems, set in stone, metal plaques and etched glass, for you to follow as you wander through the town centre, discovering its treasures. The river Test flows beneath the main street, a plaque where they intersect has a poem and I quote," fish swim where road and river meet", and indeed it is possible to see trout swimming happily in great numbers. Following one of the many paths that lead off into the countryside, it is possible to follow the river and its many tributaries for miles, although care must be taken as the land can be marshy.

Along the main street there are a number of good public houses serving good food. Having chosen a particular establishment one Sunday afternoon in search of a roast lunch, I had been pleased to find a large wingback leather armchair, at a table next to a window looking out on to the street. It had proved a perfect place from which to keep an eye on the van as she sat in the street outside, and we had made it our seat for Sunday dinner from that day forward.

Chapter 19

TOILET GENIE

When work finally came to a halt for me in Andover, we visited our favourite pub in the main street one last time. The place had been quiet of recent weeks, I think because of the recession, tonight being no exception we had this section of the bar almost to ourselves. A log fire still crackled away heartily, despite the lack of paying customers. As my darling sat on the seat opposite to my wingback chair by the window, I went to the bar for the usual pint and a half of real ale.

Having liked the place I wondered if we would ever come back, it being doubtful that work would take us that way again. Indeed the problem was that my job was not taking us anywhere in the immediate future, I had been informed a few days previously that work was in short supply, the flat I had just finished probably being the last for some time. It was now almost December, and the chance of a change to the situation before Christmas was non-existent.

Ensconced in my chair with the window to my right I kept a close eye on the van, while the log fire that crackled away to my left warmed our feet. As the year had worn on, this fire had become increasingly comforting. Indeed there had been a lot of evenings where I could have sat there for hours, but having to get up for work the following morning, we would not allow ourselves to stay late. Drinking their ale and watching the rain as it lashed against the window, this particular evening had good potential to be a four or five pint affair.

It was not that I was drowning my sorrows, for we had done well over the past months and could afford the time off. But with no work in the foreseeable future we were contemplating our funds carefully, deciding what to do. We had been to Spain twice previously, and knew that we could live there quite cheaply. The cost would be incurred travelling there and back, which costs us about five hundred euros each way. If we come through France we spend more on fuel and toll roads, if we go direct to Spain on a ferry it costs a similar amount in the end. This was only a short while after the fiasco with Lehman's bank going bust, and the recession was still a serious matter, as it would be for some time to come.

Having devoured a fine roast dinner we were eating sticky toffee pudding, and already I was on my third pint. Cursing the fact that our favourite site in Standlake closes for the winter, we were throwing ideas back and forth at one another with concerns as to where we should go. My suggestions began to be dismissed more rapidly as it became apparent that the darling was forming a plan. I finished the last of the ice cream from my sticky toffee pudding and turned my attention towards the bar and reaching the previously elusive fourth pint. When I sat back down and supplied her with another half of real ale, she came right out with it and told me we were going to the new forest.

We had visited the new forest only once previously, using it as a stop off on the way to Spain, as it is reasonably well located for the ferry port. By no means had we done the place justice, having seen very little of it. In an effort to give merit to the idea, the darling was unsuccessfully trying to remind me of the camp site we had stayed on. My mind was instantly brought into focus by the mention of a donkey behind a fence at the bottom of the site, emitting loud and painful sounding noises at the crack of dawn every morning. Suddenly I could remember the place quite well having had many more reasons to like it, and as soon as I said as much I could see that the matter had been considered settled. Quickly realising my error, in that if I wanted a fifth pint I should have feigned memory loss a few moments longer, I was verbally dragged out of my seat in no time at all.

We ran the fifty yards or so back to the van in the rain, throwing our coats in the bathroom as we climbed aboard. The drive back to the site took only a couple of minutes longer, after which I had to brave the elements for a moment to plug our mains hook-up back in. With the kettle beginning to bubble I had finished tuning in the television, while the darling referred to the relevant campsite guidebook. In line with our recollections the site was very reasonably priced indeed. We had spent only a handful of days there, and so did not really know even the immediate surroundings of the site. Having been preoccupied with our imminent departure for warmer climes, there had been little inclination to want to walk in the English cold any more than was necessary.

With curiosity well and truly aroused the little darling got our laptop out from the cupboard. As I sat patiently waiting my turn, wanting to look at google earth to ascertain our chances of some good walks, the dear girl then put her time to further good use. In the process of searching the internet she discovered that a large commercial site, a couple of hundred yards away from the site we had used on our previous visit, displayed an offer on their website detailing a fantastic reduction for anyone who booked online. Moments later we had booked ourselves in for the festive period. The offer closed just before Christmas and started again in January, for which period we would simply move the couple of hundred yards along the road to the cl we were already familiar with.

Having already had a detailed look at the website before we made our booking, we were full of anticipation to use the on-site gym and swimming pool which were both included in the price. From the photographs I could see that they were top notch. We sat with the television on for a while but neither of us was particularly interested, preferring to discuss tomorrow's journey. In order to make a good start we paid heed to the old saying," early to bed, early to rise", and sure enough the next morning found us ready to get on the road at nine o'clock, full of coffee and toast.

I followed our progress on the map as the darling drove, sticking to the route we had chosen the previous night. With my phone on the dash we could hear the voice of the sat-nav lady, helpfully informing us of upcoming roundabouts. A little over an hour's drive later we arrived at Godshill, and I remembered fondly that we had been about to leave the country the last time we had been there. Passing the turn off for the cl on which we intended to see in the New Year, we had only two hundred yards to go to reach our destination. The sat-nav began to inform us of this in its monotonous voice, so I pressed the mute button, aware that the thing was on thin ice.

Of course the usual rigmarole had to be dealt with at the reception block. We were told an area of the site in which to choose a pitch, before returning to inform them which number we had chosen. Having had a nagging doubt that there might be a problem and the discount would not apply to us I was relieved to have someone accept payment, since we had only made a booking on the laptop the night before. We are always reluctant to enter credit card details into any computer, unless it is absolutely unavoidable.

All the pitches were of a similar ilk, in that they were hard-standing, and with exception to only a few were also empty. The only things left to debate were proximity to the shower block and of course the path the sun would take in the sky, knowing that we would welcome the free heat it provides on our wind-screen. Never being ones to miss the chance of a bit of a debate we offered up opposing selections for our choice of pitch.

Knowing that my opinion on such matters had proved itself of questionable worth in the past, and becoming thoroughly fed up of being stood outside in the cold while she drove from pitch to pitch in the warmth of the van, I relinquished what small amount of say I may have had in the matter. The levelling blocks went underneath our front wheels and with us hooked up to the mains and the bike removed from the rack within seconds, we had arrived.

As requested I went back to reception and informed them of our choice of pitch for their records. A quick look inside the gym proved that everything was as good if not better than portrayed in the website, in contrast to our previous Christmas spent in the Uk when we had made the disastrous misjudgement of leaving everything to the last minute and taking the only thing we had been able to get.

I had thought about this matter as I walked back, and once inside the warmth of the van again I brought the subject up with my darling. She reminded me that our last Christmas in the UK had been prior to the recession, and we came to the conclusion that all the empty pitches were due to the fact only determined campers or those without choice would camp in England in the weather we now faced, with a white Christmas being a distinct possibility.

It still hadn't turned midday so we decided to take a walk around the site before dinner. We had a brief look at the wares on offer in the shop for future reference, finding whisky marmalade albeit at an extortionate price. Walking the sites own forest trail, contained within their expansive grounds, took us on a path through the log cabins and static caravans, before threading away into the woods. We are always prepared for a walk, even if we set off out for what is only intended to be a short stroll, we will inevitably be wearing the relevant outdoor gear and robust footwear. I had one of my jerseys I usually wear for work on beneath my outdoor coat, managing to keep me more than comfortable in the biting cold.

Through the trees the path wound down Godshill, turning back on itself every hundred yards to ease the gradient. Squirrels darted about across the path in front of us constantly, running up the trunks of the trees then jumping from tree to tree at the top as if showing off. Since our encounter with the party of hunters, with their immense falcons perched atop their wrists, the darling had become something of a twitcher, and so with various types of bird being pointed out to me we made our way down the hill.

Still skirting through the trees at the bottom of the hill, we followed the path until the trees thinned out altogether and the path began to follow the river Avon. Although cold the day was also crisp and bright, and a thin mist could be seen rising from the river in wisps. A family of swans floated along beneath the mist, providing us with more photographic opportunities than my clumsy attempts with a camera should rightfully deserve in a lifetime. The darling, in contrast, is adept with a camera and got some good shots.

Arrows and signs which had been placed strategically along the trail, now informed us that we must part company with the river and begin winding a way through the trees once more. Knowing that we were on our return journey and would soon be facing the climb up Godshill, my darling chose that moment to express a desire to visit the little girl's room, blaming the river for noisily rushing alongside us. Preparing a retort along the lines of the river having done this for innumerable years, I was struck dumb by the site of a portable toilet sat in the middle of a clearing in the woods not twenty yards away, miraculously coming into view through the trees right after my loved one had spoken.

Completely agog at my companion's ability to astound me, my mind began to search for a virtual reality crucifix it keeps at the back of a cupboard somewhere, and I could only stop and stare. With a guilty but worried look on her face, she dismissed the matter forthwith, saying she would not find such a convenience up to the relevant standard for the procedure. Unable to allay my concerns but still in disbelief, I stomped the remaining yards across to the portable toilet, as would an atheist toward a crying statue of the Madonna.

I opened the door without further ado, revealing an immaculate white porcelain toilet, and could only manage to turn round slowly as my mind raced. Unable to meet my gaze, I observed her coercing conversation toward a small robin perched atop the toilet roof, claiming it to have followed her from the top of the hill. Having grown accustomed to my little darling's mysterious and unorthodox methods, I put the matter to the back of my mind. Anyone who doubts my story though, need only walk this route themselves to verify the existence of the aforementioned convenience.

Sure enough we saw the robin again. As we walked through the woods toward the foot of the hill we encountered him twice, and having ascended the path up the other side of the hill he awaited us at the top, where we took the opportunity for photographs not only of the robin but of the view. We now saw a third route traversing the hillside, across a valley but reaching the same summit, upon which static caravans were situated with what I can only imagine being fantastic views from their large patio windows.

In the coming weeks we enjoyed this walk every day, before going to the gym in the afternoon and reading or watching television at night. We were pleased with our surroundings and decided to make the best of them while the offer was still available, as a result of which we did not venture into the new forest at all. I would go into Fordingbridge on the scooter, a journey of about five minutes, and could get anything we needed from there.

I was sat reading in one of our armchairs one afternoon, making full use of the sun coming through the windscreen, when in rolled an American rv of considerable size but old with it. Without a great deal of finesse the vehicle was eventually parked, the door opened and a man climbed out. He wore a long grey trench-type looking coat, and even from this distance I could clearly see a large object adorned with feathers hanging from his earlobe. A car had driven in moments later, and I soon gathered that a friend had driven the car on behalf of the owner of the rv. They both disappeared in the car again and after about forty minutes he returned, this time on a large motorbike again with the car following.

Talking to him a few days later I got to know him as Rueben, and found his life to be more chaotic than anyone I had encountered in a long time. He told me he had lived in his rv for a few months, and I could see that he liked the experience. He seemed to spend much of the time alone for the first few days, until his girlfriend arrived along with her teenage son and his girlfriend. I could tell they all liked a drink, having heard the unmistakeable sound of bottles being carried in and out in carrier bags on a regular basis.

One night not long before Christmas we were lying in bed reading our books, and heard the evening drinking session reach a crescendo of raised voices and foul language. Poor Rueben could be heard shouting "not my van for" something's sake, shortly after which the voices became louder, Rueben presumably having managed to eject them from his beloved van. As the argument continued outside the police were frequently mentioned by both parties, until eventually the young lad could be heard to tell his mother to come away. Before hostilities were completely ceased a loud smash was heard, like that of a window breaking.

The next morning we were sat having our post breakfast coffee when I heard a knock at our driver's door. Looking round to my right, I saw a dejected looking Rueben with a downtrodden look on his face. I opened the door and he began to apologise profusely for the disturbance of the previous night, a boulder sized hole in the windscreen of his car bearing testament to his having paid dearly for an evening drinking session. I tried repeatedly to placate his apologising telling him not to worry about it, yet he still walked away muttering apologies. We had already discussed, during a previous conversation, that the offer on the pitch fee was unavailable over Christmas, with me having told him I was moving to the cl down the road. Nice guy that he was, and I now felt a great deal sorrier for him, I was relieved that his vehicle was too big for the cl round the corner.

Chapter 20

THE NEW FOREST

On the day that we had to move to our other site around the corner, we had a leisurely breakfast knowing that we need not leave until midday. In the usual well drilled manner we had the van packed away in five minutes, leaving only the short few hundred yards drive around the corner. Pulling into the farm, I remembered the place immediately and was pleased we had decided to spend Christmas there. Behind the farm house sits a large barn, from which the owner of the site also runs a business selling feed for livestock. The caravan guidebook states the site to be unsuitable for children due to the constant movement of a forklift, which is actually used rather sporadically and makes little noise. Thus rendered a child free zone the site becomes, if possible, an even better option than before.

The darling brought the van to a halt in front of the barn and before I could get out the jolly farmer's face appeared at the passenger window, with the slightly red cheeked complexion only achieved from a lifetime working outdoors. I think he recognised my accent more than my face but was too polite to say so, and we exchanged the sort of pleasant greetings rarely seen at club sites. I paid for my pitch and he led us into the site, showing us which pitches were available as he went. We selected one at the top, knowing this to be farthest away from the donkey that lives behind a fence at the bottom of the site. He can be heard once every morning when he wakes up, but after that is quiet as a lamb.

It was now almost one o'clock so we did not walk far that day. The previous time we had stayed we left without even walking further down the lane and into Blissford, so I suppose I could also say that we broke our previous record on the first day there. Whilst we are both keen walkers I cannot lay claim to being some sort of rambler, perhaps I may walk a dozen miles including the return journey. I prefer my walks taken regular, regardless of all but the most severe weather. Feeling good to be off work and having the new forest on our doorstep we both felt that it would be somehow sacrilegious not to get out and make the most of it, and had promised ourselves we would be out every day it was possible.

As it turned out we had no cause for concerns regarding the weather, although cold the day remained bright and dry with no wind at all. Walking down the lane into Blissford we passed houses of varying sizes, discreetly hiding behind large hedges which made our attempts at nosiness a waste of time. At the bottom of the lane a small ford enables the road to cross a stream, no doubt being the source of what I must admit to be an extremely apt name. A dozen or so donkeys had gathered by the stream, seemingly oblivious to our presence and intent on foraging for food. Looking at them we both felt a bit sorry for them, and decided they should be the recipients of some of our leftovers over the coming days.

Past the donkeys we turned left, heading vaguely in the direction the stream had come from, and along a track which started to climb upwards very gradually. A few hundred yards later we were at the foot of a grassy hill, with open fields to our left beyond which the forest could be seen like a curtain drawn across the landscape. Our track now turned into a gravel path winding away out of sight and up the hill in what seemed like a gentle slope, at least to begin with. Wild ponies could now be seen almost everywhere I chose to look, sometimes seeming to follow each other round as they looked for food.

The gentle slope up the hill continued in this manner for a short way before becoming more arduous. Thankfully the forest is looked after by the national park authority and the path is kept in good condition, allowing us to take in the view as we walked without fear of losing our footing. A short climb later we reached the top of the hill and were rewarded with views for many miles around. Hills could be seen so far in the distance to our right as to be almost on the horizon, while to our left there were patches of forest, becoming thicker the further the eye wandered. From our vantage point we could see endless opportunities for walking, with paths leading off in all directions.

We found that we could either head back down the hill on the other side, where the forest awaited us on the opposing side of a valley, or we could walk the three or four miles along the flat ridge we had just ascended to and enter the forest at the far end. Alternately we could veer right to an area the map had informed us to be called Abbotswell, where the path crested another hill and vanished behind some houses. The grass had now turned into heather, with trees here and there and gorse all around, and ponies could be seen chomping away happily in all directions. The landscape warranted extensive exploring, and as darkness would soon be approaching we decided to ponder our next route as we walked home.

The festivities passed sleepily in Blissford that year. As usual we had Christmas dinner in the van, there being nowhere else I would know for certain that I would enjoy it to that extent. Duck pate was for starters, followed by a full turkey dinner with all the added extras like sausages wrapped in bacon, or pigs in blankets as they are called. To top it all off we had sticky toffee pudding followed by Christmas cake. Although the space is limited in our kitchen, the darling is able to perform miracles and has found with practise that no challenge is too big. Discounting a brief rendition of auld langsyne by some of our fellow campers on New Year's Eve, we had the luxuriously quiet festive period we had been in search of when deciding to head to the New forest.

Thankfully the weather remained dry, and we walked every day. With the help of google we discovered all the public houses in the area, trying them out in turn. I found them all to be exactly what I was looking for at the time, with open fires, real ales and good food, the deciding factor usually being which walk we wanted to do that day. On one of our favourite routes we would walk down into Blissford, then take the lane to the left and eventually climb to the top of the hill. From here we could walk all the way along the top of the hill until it joined the forest, a fantastic vantage point from which to admire the views across the valley to our right and indeed all around. Footpaths could be seen to criss-cross the landscape as far as the binoculars would allow.

At the far end of the hill we found it wise to exert caution, after stopping for sandwiches one day only to have a herd of cows come along to disturb us. The gravel path finally enters the forest, and it pleases me to say that it is no less than very well kept at any point on its journey. We encountered so few people that the path seemed to have been created solely for our exclusive use, although from time to time we did see the occasional horse and trap speeding along.

The path twists and turns through Eyeworth wood before arriving in Fritham, the furthest we would usually walk in that direction having come some seven miles walking distance from Blissford. I find it best to keep in mind that every step I take when setting off out for a walk, is an extra step I need to take to get home. With the sun shining brightly it can be easy to forget this, as we found one day in early January. We had set off a bit later than usual and taken our time, walking at our own leisurely pace. Thinking it to be a good place for a picnic, we had gotten into the habit of sitting on a couple of sawn off tree trunks that lay by the side of the track in the middle of Eyeworth wood. Indeed, once again, it seemed that they had been left there specifically for our use.

Enjoying the fresh air and with the bright rays of the sun beaming down on us, we wanted to walk further and reach Fritham. A small pub there has a fine selection of ales, brewed just down the road at Ringwood, and if I'm to be perfectly honest this acted like something of a carrot enticing me forward. It was almost possible to forget that it was winter, the exertion of the walk having seen us both unzip our jackets long before we had stopped for our picnic. Being that we were in the middle of a forest I had a very careful smoke, as I waited for the darling to finish her sandwiches. With the weight off our feet we were enjoying the rest and took the time to deliberate on whether or not to walk any further, eventually being won over by the thought of the real ale and resolving to get a taxi for the return journey if necessary.

We had our usual dosage of the local brew, a pint for me and a half for the darling, on this occasion Ringwood's Old Thumper. With its low beamed ceilings and open fire the pub could quite easily have proven difficult to withdraw oneself from, at least until we used the mobile to ring a local taxi and found he wanted seventeen pound to take us the short six or seven mile journey home. Whereas our feet were beginning to weary as we entered the pub, our reluctance to be exploited had bestowed upon us a new found energy. We managed to keep up a reasonable pace all the way through Eyeworth wood, there being nothing like the thought of being in a forest after dark to make one walk faster.

Ominously the clouds could be seen approaching as we walked back along the ridge of the hill, thus quickening our pace even further. A full seventeen pounds better off for the experience, we were soon back at the van. Although sweating I switched the heating on straight away, knowing that in the ten minutes it takes to warm the van we would be beginning to cool. Before I had even managed to get my slippers on there was a terrific clap of thunder and the heavens opened, bringing a downpour of considerable magnitude. With the heating purring away inaudibly we sat with our feet up enjoying our books, until a lightning storm provided brief entertainment.

Of course when we returned to the larger commercial site across the road, we continued to walk in every direction possible, eventually getting to know the area quite well. I had expected to see Reuben rolling in at any day, making a number of journeys on account of all his paraphernalia as he had done a couple of short weeks previously, but I never saw him again. I presumed he'd experienced such difficulty in finding an alternative site that he must have decided to stay there.

Towards the end of January we were treated to a blanketing of snow, forcing us to revert to our previous habit of the on-site forest trail, it being the only accessible option. With the on-site gym and spa at our disposal we were never short of something to occupy our time, the on-site bar and restaurant also came in handy a couple of times too. We stayed there until the end of February, and enjoyed the time in a way previously un-paralleled. All good things come to an end however, and we couldn't afford to forget about work for too long, no matter how much it seemed to have forgotten us. The trouble was that no developers were building any houses at all, due to the increasing problems of the recession, and there was no work to be had for anyone in the house-building industry.

Chapter 21

RETURN TO BRIDGEWATER

Feeling like it was time to pull our heads from the sand, I went to Ringwood job-centre at the end of February 2009, and signed on the dole. I really had exhausted all other options and the job-centres at that time were full of people in my position. We had lived off our savings for about three months now, and money was becoming tight. Sat one evening discussing our predicament we decided to, "pull our belts in" as it were. One of our biggest expenditures being pitch fees, we had the instrumental idea of moving to the cheapest pitch available.

Having made the decision we were out of bed early the next day, in order for me to go back to Ringwood job-centre and inform them. As far as they were concerned I was classed as being of no fixed abode, and I simply told them I was going in search of work, which was true anyway. I found their procedures to be something of an ordeal. I only wanted to inform them of a perfectly legitimate change of address and yet they had a multitude of questions, some of which I am sure they asked twice just to be impertinent. Soon the matter was over, and we exercised our age old human right to relocate in search of prosperity.

If our intentions were prosperous then our destination was anything but. In the short term we really needed a cheap camp site, where we could think about our predicament without seeing money draining away through our fingers. The previous evening I had made the suggestion that we return to Bridgewater, fully expecting the little darling to refuse point blank I was taken aback and somewhat aghast when she had agreed. However, seen without the darkness and fog which had presided over our previous visit two years ago, the site seemed a little better. The general impression was one of having had only the bare minimum of maintenance work done in at least the last ten years. The day was clear enough to be able to see though, that the surrounding area had a lot to offer us in the form of walks.

This time we were allocated a pitch in the long stay area, better known to me as the collection of manky caravans lurking behind the shower block. As usual we managed to park the van and have her all set up in about five minutes. During which time our new neighbour reached a point at which he could contain his curiosity no longer, and finally came out to see who we were whilst pretending to fill a water butt. Expecting him to say hello I gave him the opportunity to make eye contact but he chose not to, preferring to imagine that I did not exist. In stark contrast, a slightly unkempt looking guy emerged from a very neat and tidy looking caravan in the corner and came right over, introducing himself as John as he shook my hand.

The gym had been closed during my previous visit, so naturally I was keen to get in and have a look at it. Having gotten the code from reception I entered it into a keypad next to the door, and soon found myself the sole occupant of a decent if slightly untidy gym. Little did I know but I was to have this luxury many times during my stay, discounting that is, the fact the darling was usually with me. When that is the case however, I am under strict instruction to leave her well alone and get on with my own thing. The luxury of the situation was in the fact that we could choose our own music.

Having been unable to sample the delights of the bar the last time we were there, due to it having been closed as well, I made it my business to get in there for a pint that evening. Stood there drinking a pint of John Smiths I went pretty much unnoticed by half a dozen others, leading me to form the opinion it was no rare thing to see a stranger. None of the faces I saw were recognisable from the camp site, but having only arrived I was not sure. The place was bigger than I had expected, big enough to enable them to use it as a function room.

Over the coming days we came to know everyone by face and had already prescribed some of them their own individual monikers long before we got to know their real names, in a friendly way of course and just between ourselves. The guy next door we decided to call Fat Boy, on account of having heard him call his wife Freda and thinking the two went together well.

Directly opposite us was a shabby looking caravan with what can only be described as extensive accident damage to its front end, bearing testament to the fact it had served a long and colourful career. The occupant was a small man with glasses probably about thirty five. Every day he would get into his battered old car and drive two hundred yards up to the other end of the site, where all the pitches were empty. Having arrived at his destination he would open the door of the car and let the dog out, then sit waiting a while before letting the dog back in and driving back.

Seeing him drive in and out all day long for some reason or other, obviously never going far, we christened him Boy Racer. It soon became clear that the dog was not even his, actually belonging to his girlfriend who lived not with him as we had thought, but in her own very similar looking caravan in the far corner to which she would retreat on a regular basis when they argued. For reasons now forgotten we came to call her Loopy. With hindsight the name fits her even better now than it did at the time, with both their lives seeming to be caught in an endless loop of fighting and making up. Unfortunately Boy Racer had something of a fragile mentality at the best of times and each break up would be marked by the appearance of flashing blue lights, if not the police then an ambulance.

While washing the dishes one evening in the communal dishwashing area, something I often do rather than use my own hot water, I got into a conversation with the Boy Racer. Loopy had been back in her own caravan for over a week and he wasted no time in bemoaning the fact. Discovering we had a common interest in football I agreed to watch an upcoming match with him over a few beers, something we made a regular fixture of if there was good football to watch. He was still the proud owner of an upturned fridge he used as a table, which was in the exact same place as it had been two years ago.

Awaiting the arrival of a letter I had to go to reception one morning not long after arriving, where I made the acquaintance of Danny. He wasted no time at all in telling me that he was a recovering addict, which I initially considered to be a bit too much information. I quickly realised however, that he was simply telling me this before someone else did, and decided I liked the guy for his openness and honesty. He soon proved himself to be one of the more down to earth members of the small community of residents.

All in all they were something of a strange crowd. Out of a dozen or so caravans, there were only a couple who had jobs. The rest could be seen to malinger around the camp site all day waiting for Giro day, with the exception of Danny who worked part time whenever he could. One trench coat wearing inhabitant would disappear every time he received a Giro, leaving a trail of creditors looking for their money.

Of the couple of people who worked one was called Gary, a welder at a nearby nuclear plant. The other was a guy called Steve who was some sort of instrument mechanic. Affixed to the side of his caravan was a safari room type awning, from the roof of which a shiny metal chimney could be seen to be jutting upwards. He had installed a log burning stove into the tent part of his awning which could be used to warm the whole caravan, by leaving the window or door open. He was a very knowledgeable bloke and could seemingly turn his hand to anything. He fixed a small problem with my scooter once and among his other achievements had managed to convert a car so that it would run on cooking oil, before selling it on at a profit.

I had always wondered if the site got busier at certain times of year, and after a few short weeks I got my answer with the arrival of Easter and the holiday period. All of a sudden the place pretty much filled up over the course of a Friday afternoon, with the arrival of about three hundred campers. From time to time I would see them poke their heads round the corner, obviously wondering why these caravans lurked behind the shower block.

Then they would notice things like the discarded refrigerator and the fact that Loopy had a window missing (some kind soul had very helpfully nailed a couple of planks across the opening to keep out the rain), and their faces would adopt a puzzled expression as they turned away. Nevertheless business was obviously booming for the site owners. The bar was open every night and most afternoons. Now that a captive customer base was present, the owners opened up the small on-site shop, which turned out to be useful for certain things like newspapers and milk etc.

As frequently reported in the news at this time, many families were now taking caravanning holidays in their inability to afford the foreign holidays of yesteryear. As a direct result there were kids everywhere, whizzing around on pushbikes and doing everything they could to shatter the tranquillity of the place. It turned out that our little scrapyard behind the shower block was one of the quieter parts of the site. Thankfully a code was needed to gain entry to the gym, and we were usually undisturbed during our daily workouts. The only person that would occasionally be in there was Gary, the guy who worked as a welder at the nuclear plant.

On my way to the shop one fine morning to collect a daily paper, I happened to find the Boy Racer sat at a table outside the bar. It was just after eleven o'clock and he had obviously been keen to make a start on the days socialising. I refused a drink thinking it to be too early by far, but stopped to talk to him for a while anyway. I suspected him to be drinking in order to null the pain of Loopy's refusal to forgive him his most recent misdemeanour. Without actually offering it to me, he informed me that he was trying to sell his car for two hundred pounds. Seeing that I was completely disinterested he went on to say that he would take fifty pound.

I asked if things were really that bad, to which he cheerily replied that he wasn't too bothered, having bought the vehicle off Fat Boy and still owing him the money for it. Things were bad he told me, when he had first arrived on the site almost a year ago, as he had lived in a tent at that time. I couldn't help but think that the worst thing to have happened to him was meeting Loopy. As we spoke I could see her, about twenty yards away, trying to charm one of the campers into buying her a drink. Sensing that things could turn nasty I bade him farewell, and as I left him he began to talk to two young ladies who were stood nearby, in a valiant but utterly unsuccessful attempt to make Loopy as jealous as he was.

At times we had some good weather that year, in spring of 2009. With no improvement in the employment situation we made good of our time there, going to the gym every morning and walking in the surrounding countryside most afternoons. Someone had told us of an old castle in the small neighbouring village of Stogursey, and seeing the sun shining down the following Saturday we decided to go and look for it. With some sandwiches and a flask of tea in my rucksack, we set off out in our waterproof coats, just in case.

Following the road as it snaked its way through the rolling landscape of the Somerset countryside, we encountered almost no traffic at all. For some of the way the road was lined by high hedgerows, whereas at other points there were trees here and there. The undulating nature of the landscape provided few vantage points from which to take in a good view of the immediate area, and as if in compensation for this, the Quantock hills were standing proudly in the distance as an ever present reminder of where we were.

Stogursey being quite a small place we soon found the aforementioned castle, sat on the very edge of the village. I could not help but wonder about how the place would have looked in the past, with the thickness of the walls clearly visible it had obviously been heavily fortified, although it must have been quite small for a castle. Walking around the moat in a complete circle, we were able to see beyond the ruins of the old walls, and into what is now the garden of a small house built where the gatehouse would have been and accessed by a small bridge. Later research on the internet has taught me that the bridge is part of the original structure built in the thirteenth century, when one William de Courcy made it his base, somehow the local dialect mutating this and giving the village its name. According to Wikipedia the castle played a small part in the wars of the roses, after which it fell into disrepair and has lain in ruins ever since.

Unable to gain access to the grounds of the ruined castle we contented ourselves with a view from a nearby grassy bank, as we sat and enjoyed our sandwiches. As is so often the case when I visit such old buildings, I found myself wondering how many things had occurred here over the centuries that had escaped anyone's attempts at recording them, thus becoming forgotten by all except the old castle itself. Although the day was by no means warm the sun continued to shine brightly in a sky that was pleasantly bereft of cloud cover, and I drained my flask of tea while sat on the grass having a smoke.

In passing an old church on the way through the village, we had happened to see a sign proclaiming there to be a jumble sale in progress. Never being able to pass up the chance to have a good scavenge through old books we spent an hour or so hunting for a good read, being careful not to buy too much as it would have to be carried home. I had worked on the assumption of yielding worthy results and I was not disappointed, the local community obviously having its fair share of avid readers.

Once the bookshelves had been exhausted we decided to take five minutes rest in the small tea room, where a delightful old girl who was dressed in a pinafore treated us to a free cup of tea when we bought cake from her. Subsequently carrying almost as much weight in cake as I was in books, but with an impressive view of the Quantocks now directly in front of us to displace the fact from our minds, we found the walk home just as pleasing as we had done setting off out to find the castle.

By the time May arrived in 2009, we had spent almost three months on Bridgewater. It had been hard to imagine at one point, but one day the phone rang and I was asked to return to work the following Monday. Faced with the prospect of going back to the daily grind, it now began to dawn on us both what we would have to leave behind. No more leisurely workouts at the gym in the morning, and no more walking in the sunny afternoons.

It had become so hit and miss in the construction industry, making it difficult to earn money, that I had contemplated leaving the industry for good and finding some other means of earning a living. In the end we decided it better to go back to what we know, and if the work transpired to only last a short while we would cross that hurdle when we came to it. Within an hour of having received the call we had packed everything away into the relevant storage compartments and were ready to leave. The other long term residents had never seen anyone uproot themselves so quick. We said our goodbye's and drove straight to the local supermarket, in order to fill the cupboards of the van with essentials.

Chapter 22

THE DAY WE CAUGHT THE TRAIN

When I got back to Overton the site agent told me that the houses had been dramatically reduced in price by almost two hundred thousand pounds, in the hope of getting someone to buy them. We had taken a detour into Swindon on the way over and been quite shocked at what we had found, with many of the sites containing unfinished properties with temporary roofs and windows boarded up. Meanwhile back on the top of Watership Down nothing had changed at all, except perhaps there were a few more campers than we had previously encountered. We replaced our walks in the Somerset countryside with walks in the Hampshire countryside, but our regular workouts at the gym every morning were to be sorely missed for quite some time.

The economy was stuttering in its recovery, henceforth the construction industry was also stopping and starting. At one point my supervisor came to see me one Monday morning, and told me there would be no more work until the following Monday. Always able to make a good situation out of a bad one, within the hour we had the van all packed up and were off down the A303 heading to Cornwall. It always feels good to be setting off somewhere at Monday dinnertime, when the roads are quiet and everyone else is just starting their weeks work. On that particular occasion however, things were short lived, as the company rang on Wednesday as we were just setting off out for a walk on Bodmin moor. Unfortunately I was back at work the next day, and we had driven all the way down to Cornwall for a couple of days and half a walk.

Things continued in this fashion for quite a while, and we made the best of many half days at work by getting out for a walk in Watership Down country. With fond memories of our time in the

New Forest the previous year, and with the added burden of slight financial turbulence, we had decided to forego on our excursion to Spain for the second year running. The winter had been very mild the year before, and as time wore on we became accustomed to the idea of going back to the New Forest. Then in November work sent me to Alton, close to the historic town of Winchester.

For the first time ever, it began to seem like our caravan guidebooks were going to let us down. We had always managed to find a camp site near to where I would be working, usually within five to ten miles. An internet search yielded nothing in the specific area we needed to be in either. In the end we decided to go to a pub cl we had noticed in the nearby village of Binstead, earlier having dismissed it on account of there being no electric hook up facilities available. Knowing that we would have to be slightly economical with the vans batteries in the absence of a power supply, we decided to pull in late on Sunday night.

The sat nav came in useful once again, it being easy to miss a turn off on the small country lanes our destination dictated we would have to traverse. Feeling like we had driven considerably further than what the guidebook had informed us we would have to, we at last found the pub in the middle of the small village of Binstead. Pulling into the car park at the back we saw a small field surrounded by pine trees. I wished we had been sent there during summer, as the field looked the perfect place to get our awning out and sit having a beer after finishing work. Winter was now upon us so we elected to stay on the tarmac of the car park, knowing that if it rained the van might become stuck on the field. We went through our well drilled routine which sees us fully set up within five minutes of arrival at a new site, and turned our attention toward the pub.

A large pile of cut logs sat outside the door indicating the presence of an open fire so we wasted no time in locking the van and heading inside. I suspected the man behind the bar to be the landlord as soon as I saw him, and this proved to be the case when he greeted us. Pubs were struggling a bit at the time, due to the recession and the newly enforced smoking ban, and there were only a few other customers in that evening.

Having paid for our pitch we got a pint and a half of real ale then sat at the side of the blazing fire, the heat being too intense to sit in front. A wave of relief flooded over us, for at one point we thought we weren't going to find a pitch near enough to where I would be working. While sat enjoying our ale we had a look through the menu and, upon finding the pricing extremely reasonable, decided to go back in Wednesday evening for a bite to eat. I put the case that this would effectively save us some of the charge in the vans batteries, and sure enough when Wednesday's meal proved to be more than what was expected we made it a regular event.

The weather had taken a very icy turn for the worse, meaning I had to exert caution while on the scooter going to work in the morning. At weekends we would drive elsewhere, usually booking a pitch on a larger site and so enabling ourselves to do our laundry while also charging the van and filling the water tank. Historic Winchester was just a few miles away and on more than one occasion we made use of the caravan club site there. The weather had become too cold for walking so we contented ourselves with wandering the town centre on Sunday afternoon, waiting for some establishment or other to catch our eye, beckoning us inside for a pint and a roast dinner.

Our National Trust membership came in handy yet again allowing us to visit Hinton Ampner, an elegant country house near Alresford which is under the ownership of the trust. By luck there was a hand bell ringing rehearsal as we were there, and as they went through various Christmas carols some of the more enthusiastic visitors burst into song, giving the house a festive feeling I thought only attainable in black and white movies. Stood silently at the back and just listening, I felt glad that work had brought us to the area, there being so much worthy of visiting in our wonderful country that it is easy to see why such little gems are often overlooked.

As I have said before we always try and see any attractions in the area's we visit, not knowing if we will ever return. The nearby steam railway known as the Watercress line had therefore sat on our to-do list since we had arrived, until one day early in December when we parked the van at Alton train station for the afternoon. The whole place had been decorated in period, with advertisements for products long since unavailable adorning the walls amongst various other memorabilia scattered here and there.

In contrast to modern contraptions the train arrived bang on time, and once aboard the genuine old steam train we found it to be remarkably comfortable inside, in spite of its considerable age. As steam billowed past our window the train trundled along the track, stopping only briefly at Medstead and Ropley, until reaching Alresford where we were afforded time to walk into the small market town for a bite to eat before the return journey.

Even with hindsight I can forgive myself now for thinking that, as we entered the final working week before Christmas, I would be staying at the same job for the remainder of the year. Unseen forces were conspiring against us though, and a bizarre chain of events concerning the company I was working for, led to some surplus materials having been delivered to the site in Overton which we had left a few weeks earlier. I had been asked to go there on Thursday and Friday, to do a couple of other small jobs with the main objective being to get the consignment of plasterboards indoors before the holiday period and thus protected from the elements. As such, Wednesday found us not settled by the fireside of the pub enjoying our supper, but making the short journey back to Watership Down.

The rest, as they say, is history. Man makes plans and god laughs.

Chapter 23

ROLLS ROYCE MAGNOLIA

Late Summer 2010. Not far from London.

Forsaking the comfort of my armchair in order to go to work in the morning, is a task made easier for me by the fact that my darling gets out of bed to make my breakfast and a packed lunch. Perchance this is because we live in a small van and without her assistance I make such a degree of noise as to render sleep impossible, but being the main beneficiary of the arrangement I never question the matter.

I stepped out of the van one particularly dank and drizzly Friday morning with her words ringing in my ears, causing me to stifle a chuckle. Feeling my eyes on her behind as she crawled back beneath the covers, she guiltily returned my glance and said she was going back to bed because it was her "last day". After thirty minutes during which she prepared an unusually meagre packed lunch (due to the cupboards being empty by Friday) and a paltry breakfast (due to a few gin and tonics on Thursday evening), I came to the conclusion that, in her eyes, the weekend started right here.

Taking care not to make excessive noise with our outdoor storage cupboards as I extracted my work tools, I quickly donned my waterproof clothing and pushed the scooter a safe distance from the van before starting the engine. My trusty steed had been spluttering of late, at times sounding distinctly like the proverbial bag of spanners it had begun to visually resemble after a number of years spent ferrying me back and forth to various building sites. When it had made it through the previous winter, albeit with a few extra quid invested to keep it rolling, I had naively thought it was good for the rest of the year.

Five hundred metres later I approached the main gate of the site, the last vestiges of power dissipating from beneath me as though the thing had an empty fuel tank. In the absence of any more advanced mechanical knowledge I removed the petrol cap, certain in my mind that the tank was not in need of replenishment. Sure enough there was petrol sloshing about aplenty, meaning the problem required attention beyond my abilities.

Returning my crash helmet to its home beneath the seat of the scooter, I pulled up the hood of my waterproofs to gain some protection from a down pouring which had grown in magnitude along with the darkness of my mood. Stood by the side of the road, I contemplated waking the darling from her slumber with a legitimate reason for my return, when the sight of a familiar vehicle caught my eye as it came around the roundabout that the site gate opened onto.

A blue transit is by no means a rare sight on the roads, but when I caught a glimpse of a scruffy looking individual with long hair and sunglasses on in spite of the inclement weather, I knew it could only be one person. I raised my arm in recognition and an attempt to give him no opportunity to drive past, and sure enough he screeched to a halt in the opening of the site entrance. Known to me only as "dazzler", which was how he had introduced himself when we first met, the occupant of the van rolled down his window and greeted me with a smile that turned to a grimace as his mouth tried to keep hold of a rolled up cigarette. Fortunately I was on the route to and from work of this fellow builder who, by chance, was working on the same site.

I pushed the scooter onto a grass verge by the side of the road, before climbing into the passenger side of dazzler's van with my rucksack by my feet. Knowing that my darling would be in a state of shock if she discovered my scooter to be abandoned at the side of the site entrance, I rang to inform her of my change in predicament, foregoing on the possibility of incurring her wrath by giving her a wake-up call. When she questioned whether it would be ok left parked there for the rest of the day I could only respond that it would be a blessing if someone pinched it.

Relief washed over me as our arrival at the building site signalled an end to the assorted tales dazzler had spent the journey regaling me with. Accompanying me from the car park into site, he pulled what had once been a shopping trolley (of the type used by old ladies) from the back of his van and used a bungee rope to fasten an assortment of considerably old and extremely unsafe looking tools to it. Thanking my lucky stars that at least one person had a life many times more chaotic and complex than my own, I told him I would find him at the end of the shift and finally made a start on the day's work.

At ten o'clock I stopped for a well-earned cup of tea. Sitting on the scaffold outside of the flat I was working in, I was afforded shelter from the rain by the scaffold of the flat above, and so would often choose this place as a means of getting some fresh air and a brief change of scenery. Although nothing special, this did allow me a view across the field adjacent to the old folk's home we were building, a view which began to transform before my very eyes, with the arrival of a travelling fairground. Even the weather began to turn a corner, brightening for them as they made the place their own.

As I sat there drinking the last of my tea, I realised how life had begun to change for me. We had set off five years previously with grand intentions of spending more time in the sun than previously thought possible. Due to the recession I had now missed going to Spain for two years in a row and I felt that my life was becoming like dazzler's, constantly chasing round after work in a state of chaos. My faithful scooter had died on me that morning, and even the upholstery of our beloved van was starting to show signs of wear and tear, along with various other small jobs that needed attending to.

Discussing the matter with my darling that night we realised that the previous winter, trapped in the snow on the top of a hill in Berkshire, had taken something out of the both of us, as well as our van and my scooter. We were determined to make it to Spain at the end of the year whatever happened. With summer drawing to a close and, knowing that it would take time to arrange someone we could trust to work on the van for us, we decided to divert our attention in that direction forthwith.

Replacing my scooter was a simple matter. We simply went to a dealership in Oxford and, having found the bike to be reliable before old age set in, I traded it in for a brand new one the same make and model but in white. The van was a different matter entirely. Constant searching of the internet proved to be something of a waste of time. Numerous times we would find that the people with the best websites had very little to offer by way of experience working on motorhomes, often seeming to be trying to cash in on a gap in the market and trying to exploit people such as ourselves. On one occasion we had driven all the way to Exeter to find this out.

At the other end of the scale we spoke to someone who obviously had a wealth of experience. A large RV belonging to a world famous formula one driver sat outside of his premises, giving a clue to the sort of price he would be intending to charge us for his time. Nearing the end of our tether, we rang the small garage just outside of Sheffield where we had bought the van all those years ago. We had thought all along that if all other avenues yielded such poor results we would take the long drive back up north.

My spirits sank as soon as the phone was answered, when the guy told me that the company had gone out of business some time ago.

It turned out, however, that he had previously been employed there and was now hiring the premises in order to do small pieces of work privately. After a quick description of what we required he offered to help us out, even getting a colleague to do the upholstering for us. When we arrived there the next day and met him, it turned out to be the very guy who had stopped the traffic for us as we drove the van out of the showroom and headed for my mother's house.

Over the years I had often said to my darling that if ever things got a bit too much we would simply book into a hotel for a week and leave the van in their car park. When faced with the opportunity, the dear girl who had previously been something of a professional at scouring the internet to find the best available deals on hotel accommodation, wasted no time at all in booking us into a static caravan in Blackpool. When we collected the van almost a week later, looking like something out of star trek with its seats freshly clad in Rolls Royce magnolia leather, we were both left in no doubt whatsoever that the only way really is motorhoming.

Since then we have always spent winter in Spain, where Christmas gets better every year.

TO BE CONTINUED…………………..

EPILOGUE

As you know the world is still suffering the effects of the recession, and it's entirely feasible that we could still be saying so in another five years. Getting down from the heady heights of Watership Down proved a turning point for us that year. Since then we have spent every Christmas in Spain. Pleasant memories of the previous year spent walking in the New Forest had instilled in us a sense of invincibility that was shattered in 2009 on the top of that hill, during the coldest winter for many years.

We've moved on from la marina and we now stay at the Camping Marjal Eco Resort Costa Blanca, a whopping fifteen miles away from la marina itself. With eighteen hundred pitches, I have heard it said that it is the biggest campsite in Europe, although it is not full at the moment. With any luck the peace and quiet will last for some time yet.

If you have enjoyed reading this, watch the movie. Search for "The Only Way Is Motorhoming" on youtube.

Thank you for reading.

 J.R.A. Van Duellere

5339997R00081

Printed in Great Britain
by Amazon.co.uk, Ltd.,
Marston Gate.